Montana Star Quilts
by Linda Parker

Copyright 1997
Montana Quilts, Inc.
P.O. Box 165, Helena, MT 59624
All rights reserved.

cover and design by Q Communications Group, Helena, MT

PRINTING HISTORY: First edition: September, 1997
ISBN 0-9659391-0-3

Additional copies of this publication and wholesale orders can be obtained by contacting the publisher at the above address.

Cover photo: Kaleidescope Star quilt, original design made by Linda Parker.

Montana Star Quilts

✳

Linda Parker

by Linda Parker

Introduction by Jeanne Oyawin Eder

Montana Quilts, Inc., Helena, Montana

＊

Montana Star Quilts is dedicated
to my grandmother, Florence
Vande Sandt, and to my children,
Jennifer, Jami and Josh: you are
the warp and woof of my life, you
are my inspiration and my reason
for living.

Fort Peck Reservation, maker unknown, give-away quilt

Acknowledgements

✳

A special thanks to Jerry Belgarde and John and Brooke Flynn, who worked out the templates for the Eagle Star. They otherwise would not have been included, as each Indian woman's design is her own and duplication is discouraged. Jerry has designed several Eagle variations; the particular quilt in this book was made just for me.

Thanks to *Lady's Circle Patchwork Quilts* which published an article about my Indian quilts and this book. Thanks to each person who ordered a copy and patiently waited for its completion —your support was essential to the completion of the project.

The life of this book has spanned nearly 20 years. It became a reality in 1990 when a dear friend, Robert A. Schatz, and I started Montana Quilts, Inc. Bob died in 1993 and I am eternally grateful to him for his substantial contribution to this book. Thank you to his heirs for allowing me to buy Montana Quilts, Inc.

Thanks to Anne Pincus, John Cartan, Betsy Brazy, Virginia Cochran, Alice V. Wong and Tom Ritter. Because of you, I was able to buy Montana Quilts, Inc. and finish this book. Thank you! Thank you! *Thank you!*

A special thanks to the people who worked on the book: Marilyn Evans, Amy Budde, Fong Hom, Marie Hoeffner and Beverly Magley. Thanks to Virginia Cochran and Andrew McKean, my wonderful friends and final editors. Thanks to Marty Lord for illustrations; Q Communications Group for design and layout; Craig Sharpe photographer; Biff Karlyn for illustrations and constant support; Mike Danzer, my accountant; Maureen Shaughnessy, for photo help; Troy Holter, the proofreader.

Thank you to the Montana Historical Society, Jack Kober, John Melcher, Sr., Kenneth Ryan, Dean Williams, Myron Miller and Governor Marc and Teresa Racicot for photo contributions. I'd also like to acknowledge my parents, Marj and Max Bourne; Almira Jackson; Brigit Fast Horse; Eddie Barbeau; Jeanne Eder; Pat and Jack Larmoyeux; Mike Marlow, the computer wizard; Linda Jackson for buying the very first Bitterroot pattern; and J. for helping to keep it all together—for a little while.

To the one I love, *because of you,* I have done things I didn't believe I could. You've serendipitously affected my life in ways I did not know were possible, and moved me in directions no other human being has. You are my mentor *and* my nemesis. *Thank you!*

Star quilts have always given me a focus. Originally this was going to be a book exclusively of my own designs. Discovering the importance of star quilts within the Indian culture enchanted me and once I became aware of their central role, the vital creativity of Indians became the foundation of this book.

Fort Peck Reservation, maker unknown, give-away quilt, green satin

Table of Contents

✳

Fort Peck Reservation, made by Almira Jackson. Presented to Linda Parker.

Introduction

❋

This book is the creation of Linda Parker. I first met Linda in 1991, when she called me regarding her work on Indian star quilts. I decided to drive the 500-mile round trip to Helena, Mont., to meet her and talk about her project.

My first step was to get to know her. Although Linda is a non-Indian she was raised near the Rocky Boy's Reservation in north central Montana. She later moved to Billings, where she began quilting with Jerry Belgarde, an enrolled member of the Fort Peck Reservation. Since then, she has spent 14 years of her life quilting with Jerry's continuing friendship and guidance.

Linda's vision for this project dares to look at a medium of exchange between Indian and non-Indian women. The Indian women in Montana—particularly the Sioux and Assiniboine women of the Fort Peck and Fort Belknap reservations—first became interested in the making of star quilts in the early 1900s. The Dakota Presbytery sent missionaries among the Indian people, and it was the female missionaries who set up quilting societies. The Indian women obviously saw this as an opportunity to adapt the making of star quilts into a culturally useful item.

The star quilt of today is a connection to history bridging time, just as with the buffalo robes of the last century. In the old days, before European trade goods, Plains Indians painted diamond designs on buffalo robes. These robes were valuable and considered gifts of honor. Subsequently, the star quilt became the honored gift of contemporary Indian culture. Linda's story forms a small part of that history.

Linda Parker has studied with some of the best Indian quilters alive, and her book has been a long personal struggle that honors them and the lessons they have taught her. She has made every effort to credit the Indian women who are her teachers. Her own work is a reflection of their gifts to her.

Jeanne Oyawin Eder

Fort Peck Reservation, maker unknown, give-a-way quilt. Presented to and loaned by Dean Williams.

Journey

This book speaks in honor of, and with great respect for, the Indian star quilters of Montana and the Northern Plains. These quilters deserve recognition and attention, not only for the quilts they make, but also for their ability to create them with generally limited resources. Some of these women have led very difficult lives while others have been quite successful. Rich or poor, they all share the ability, each by her own method, to create some of the most beautiful quilts ever made.

Why is there so little written information about star quilts? Indian culture has traditionally valued an oral exchange of information, and Indian star quilters still share their techniques verbally. Also, they tend to work alone, though they occasionally share hand quilting after creation of the quilt top. For these reasons, the information presented here is only an introduction to Indian star quilting. This book explores the significance of Indian star quilts, and gives you directions for eleven different designs.

***

My journey with star quilts began in 1976 in Havre, Montana, when I discovered my grandmother's 1937 Needlecraft Supply Company flier advertising three star quilts. I told my grandmother, Florence Vande Sandt, that I was going to make a star quilt. Quickly she told me I was not—it would be too difficult for my first quilt. But it's my nature not to listen when someone tells me I can't do something, and minutes later I was cutting templates from plastic lids from Schwann's ice cream buckets. I then proceeded to cut hundreds of diamonds in an array of different colors. I spent days and days arranging and rearranging diamonds on the living room floor before even attempting to sew them. Finally, I decided to be satisfied with a particular combination of colors.

Then the sewing of the diamonds began. Needless to say, they did not stay sewn together very long —I ripped them apart several times. There were moments I wanted to give up or quit, but I would not be defeated. I learned a lot making this first star quilt, including how many wrong ways there are to sew diamonds together. There were several times I wanted to cry.

Of course, I didn't know the diamonds were the incorrect degree until I was in the process of sewing the final two sections of the quilt together. I discovered I had a seven-point star instead of an eight-point star — talk about disillusion! I swore I'd never make another star quilt. My Grams helped me improvise by appliqueing the seven points onto a sheet, which was then folded and placed in a drawer for years. Soon after this initial try, I cut new diamond templates for a second attempt, being extremely cautious about the 45° angles this time. (The first quilt was made with 53° diamonds and a box of them is still around somewhere.) I probably made between 30 and 40 tied star quilts those first three years—each with a different diamond arrangement within the star. Most of these quilts were either sold for just a little more than the cost of fabric, or else given away.

In 1979 I moved to Billings, Montana, and met Pat Larmoyeux, who owned the local quilt shop. Pat allowed me to lay out bolts of fabric on the floor, and for hours on end consider color combinations. She gently encouraged me to quit using mostly prints, which tended to hide

Billings, Montana, original design by Jerry Belgarde, Feather Star

mismatched diamond intersections and also made the quilts look gaudy. Pat also recommended hand quilting instead of tying—only it seemed far too time consuming. I tried it on a small embroidered quilt and it took forever.

A profound event occurred at this time that changed my perception of star quilts forever. Pat encouraged me to go see a display of star quilts at Northern Plains, an Indian craft store. There, appearing to radiate off the walls, were the most incredibly beautiful Indian-made star quilts. I was awe-struck! After five years making star quilts, this was the first time I had seen any made by Indians. Audrey Belgarde, who worked at Northern Plains, introduced me to her mother, Jerry Belgarde, one of the quilt makers. Jerry is a Turtle Mountain Chippewa who was raised on Fort Peck, an Assiniboine and Sioux reservation in northeastern Montana. Because of our mutual interest in making star quilts, Jerry and I spent many long hours quilting and talking. From her I learned a great deal about Indian star quilting traditions.

In the fall of 1982, my stepfather, Max, ordered 16 burgundy-and-cream star quilts (he eventually bought 23!). I suspected it might take a lifetime to complete this project. After finishing two quilts of the initial design, which contained the letters "M" and "T" in each of the eight points, I contacted Jerry. When I told her my intention was to make each quilt identical, her reaction was that it would be too monotonous, and that each quilt should be unique. Jerry encouraged me to make each one different. She drew a rough sketch of a basic Fast Star point and explained how to put it together. She told me to elaborate on my own star variations using the Fast Star. By this time I had already made various arrangements of Lone Star and Broken Star quilts, and knew their potentials and their limitations. The Fast Star presented virtually limitless possibilities. I first made half a Fast Star, which is actually a Rolling Star, then nine Fast Star points into each Lone Star point. I used Fast Star points in the Broken Star and also rearranged Fast Star points with Flying Swallows. To my amazement and delight, placing wrong colors in the wrong places at the wrong time ended up enhancing the designs.

Then Jerry shared with me the simplicity of making an Indian-style quilt frame, which she places on some custom sawhorses designed by her son, Steve (the ultimate prankster), who made them to fit Jerrys tiny body. The quilt is entirely stretched out, on this frame then quilted from the outside into the center, rolling the top boards as needed. Assiniboine quilter Almira Jackson uses another interesting method — suspending her frame from the ceiling. Still other quilters have been known to use the top of a kitchen table to support the frame.

Jerry also taught me to quilt Indian style, meaning that it is not essential for the quilting stitches to be 8-to-12 per inch, so long as they are even and the piecing is done perfectly. Once the quilt is on the frame, the object is to quilt until your done or you drop, whichever comes first! Jerry came to this conclusion after her friend Brigit Fast Horse coerced her into staying up almost until morning completing her first quilt. Jerry said that for a long time she believed that once you placed the quilt on the frame and began quilting you did not stop until the quilting was absolutely finished. Later, she realized the reason for this excruciatingly wretched practice was that after several hours of quilting, your fingers get too stiff and sore to quilt the next day.

As the years passed quilting with Jerry, my knowledge of Indian star quilt traditions grew, a piece at a time. It wasn't long before I became aware that one should show sincerity in one's desire to learn by commitment and payment for skills learned. The payment differs from the white cultural norm in that it does not need to be money; rather it is something of value to the person teaching in exchange for the assistance generously given. For example, Jerry would accept items such as a quilt batt or a few yards of my fabric that she liked after spending several hours with me hand quilting my quilts.

Fort Peck Reservation, made by Brigit Fast Horse, give-away quilt

Fort Peck Reservation, made by Brigit Fast Horse, give-away quilt

Fort Peck Reservation, maker unknown. Broken Star/Tulip Quilt. Presented to Jack Kober in 1977, at memorial feast for the brother of Helen Ricker, Lakota Sioux, Poplar, Montana.

The first star quilt Jerry made was when her daughter Audrey, Red Star Woman, was chosen to be the Red Bottom Pow-wow Princess. The Red Bottom Pow-wow, an annual Assiniboine celebration, is held on the Fort Peck Reservation the third weekend of June. For this ceremonial event, as with others, the celebration committee selects a young Indian woman to preside, according to Jeanne Oyawin Eder, a Santee Sioux who taught Native American Studies at Eastern Montana College. As the selected or honored woman she is designated "Princess," a position she holds for one year. The woman should be young, a virgin, worthy, dependable and able to get along well with others. After her selection, her family is obligated to host a give-away in her behalf, star quilts being among the many gifts given.

✳

The Give-away

Star quilts are a vital element within present day Northern Plains Indian culture. The star quilt's connection to the give-away is intriguing in that it has become an ethnic symbol as integral to Indian tribes as buffalo robes were to their ancestors. Among nearly all Northern Plains tribes star quilts, commonly called star blankets, are considered one of the most honorable and prestigious items a family can give or receive.

A give-away is an honoring ceremony, or a way of saying thank you to the Creator for bestowing good fortune. It is expected in many instances for a family to "give-away" in honor of personal achievement as well as for births, naming and puberty ceremonies, basketball tournaments, graduations, homecoming ceremonies for veterans, election to a tribal office or as a pow wow official, deaths, and so forth. In the event of a death, for example, besides being given away, a star quilt can be draped over the casket at a funeral, or hung on the wall behind it. Before burial, a star quilt can be used to wrap the deceased's body or be laid beside the body.

One year after a death, a give-away is held in honor of the deceased. As part of the give-away, a feast of traditional foods such as fry bread, chokecherry soup (pudding), turnips, peppermint tea, sage hens, Indian tacos, dried meats and pemmican is prepared by the family. Star quilts are given away by family members to their friends and to friends of the deceased.

For an event such as a death give-away, the entire family or clan may participate in the preparations. In Indian culture, a clan generally consisted of a chief and all of his relatives, including adopted members. Interestingly, wealth among Plains Indians is judged by the size of the family and how much they give away. The larger the family, the wealthier they are considered. Star quilts are both given and received by people being honored.

Probably the most contemporary use of the star quilt is found at basketball tournaments. Many Indian basketball team members give star quilts to others participating in the tournament, including announcers, referees, coaches and players from other teams. Some extremely creative quilts are seen at these games, since competition among the quilt makers to produce the most outstanding one is intense.

The star quilt has also become an important display item. It is used much like a flag or banner at many family and community gatherings. Star quilts can be seen draped over cars and floats in parades, hanging on the walls of auditoriums for competitive events, and carried over the shoulders of male dancers without traditional dress. Star quilts composed of red white and blue

Fort Peck Reservation, maker unknown, Military, give-away quilt, satin

Fort Peck Reservation, maker unknown, Military, give-away quilt, satin

Fort Peck Reservation, maker unknown, Military, give-away quilt, satin

Fort Peck Reservation, made by Almira Jackson, baby quilt

Fort Peck Reservation, maker unknown, Warbonnet, satin. Presented to and loaned by Govenor Marc Raciot.

Fort Peck Reservation, maker unknown, give-away quilt. Presented to and loaned by Govenor Marc Raciot.

Fort Peck Reservation, maker unknown, give-away quilt

are made exclusively for veterans. Star designs decorate shawls, jackets and other clothing. They are also used at Yuwipi ceremonies, where the dead are summoned to find lost objects and assist in healing.

Often a star quilt is simply given as an expression of friendship. Kenneth Ryan, an Assiniboine born and raised on the Fort Peck Reservation and a former Tribal Chairman, tells us that the giving of a star quilt wishes the receiver warmth, love and a long and happy life in the same way the Creator gives you another day to live. Star quilt recipients may wrap the blanket around themselves in times of sorrow, knowing that the quilt was made for them out of friendship and love, and in this way they can find comfort. John Lame Deer, a Lakota Sioux medicine man raised on the Rosebud Reservation in South Dakota, had a star quilt made by his grandmother for his first vision quest in 1919. In the book *Lame Deer Seeker of Visions,* by John (Fire) Lame Deer and Richard Erdoes, Lame Deer said, "Sioux men are not afraid to endure hunger, thirst and loneliness, and I was only ninety-six hours away from being a man. The thought was comforting. Comforting, too, was the warmth of the star blanket which old man Chest had wrapped around me to cover my nakedness. My grandmother had made it especially for this, my first hanblechia—my first vision-seeking. It was a beautifully designed quilt, with a large morning star made of many pieces of brightly colored cloth. That star was so big it covered most of the blanket. If Wakan Tanka, the Great Spirit, would give me the vision and the power, I would become a medicine man and perform many ceremonies wrapped in that quilt. I am an old man now and many times a grandfather, but I still have that star blanket my grandmother made for me. I treasure it; someday I will be buried in it."

✳

The Morning Star and the Sacred Circle

It is not entirely clear just why the star quilt and its uses have grown in importance. The many customs surrounding the star quilt as an important give-away or display item could have arisen because of its resemblance to the morning star or its relationship to the sacred circle.

The star quilt's close identity with the morning star, known as "anpo wicahpi" in the Sioux language, is significant. The morning star stands between darkness(ignorance) and light (knowledge). It leads to understanding. The morning star also represents the direction that spirits of the dead take to travel to earth signifying a continuing link between the living and the dead. Kenneth Ryan recounts that in the old days when his people still lived in camps, the women would get up early, when the morning star came out, to tend the fires and cook breakfast. It was told that if you saw the morning star, the Creator had given you another day to live, and you would not die during that day whether gathering food, hunting or in battle.

In the book Black Elk Speaks by John G. Neihardt, Black Elk, an Oglala Sioux medicine man, advised, "Who sees the Morning Star shall see more, for he shall be wise." Then, lifting the eagle feather, he said, "This means Wakan Tanka (the Great Mysterious One); and it also means that our thoughts should rise high as the eagles do." After having a vision, Black Elk said, "I always got up very early to see the rising of the daybreak star. People knew I did this, and many would get up to see it with me, and when it came, we said, 'Behold the star of understanding.'"

The star quilt's resemblance to the Sacred Circle—a symbol painted on some buffalo robes — perhaps also has given it great significance. The Sacred Circle symbol represents the continuous cycle of all living things.

Fort Peck Reservation, maker unknown. Presented to Kenneth Ryan,
Fort Peck Tribal Chairman 1985–1987. John Reddy photo

Made by Christine Youngman, His Black Horse. Presented to Kenneth Ryan,
Fort Peck Tribal Chairman 1985–1987. John Reddy photo

Photo courtesy of the Montana Historical Society. This quilt was a gift of Kenneth and Sylvia Ryan in memory of Fort Peck Sioux leader Gerald Red Elk, in honor of NAES College, the Fort Peck Study Site and the Assiniboine and Sioux peoples of the Fort Peck Tribal Executive Board.

Fort Peck Reservation, maker unknown, give-away quilt

Photo courtesy of the Montana Historical Society. This painted buffalo robe is probably Mandan or Hidatsa from Fort Berthold, Dakota Territory, 1850–1880, collected by H. M. Cosier, an early trader at the fort.

The Oglala Sioux believe the circle is sacred because the Creator has made most things in nature round. The sun, earth, moon, planets, trees, flowers and the bodies of animals and human beings are made round. Everything that breathes and grows from the earth is round. The circle is timeless and flowing, with continuous beginnings and endings.

The life of a person also seems to move in a circle. A child learns from his elders, and when the elders die, their teachings live on in their children. The circle symbol also marks the boundary of the earth and the path of the four winds that roam the earth. The earth and the moon travel in a circle making the circle the symbol of a year. The circle has become a symbol of divisions of time and, therefore, the symbol of eternity. According to the Sioux, since the Great Spirit has caused things to be round, human beings should see the circle as sacred, as a symbol of everything created.

Another Indian leader has reminded us of the connection of star quilts to the sacred circle. Eddie Barbeau, an Objiway chief and medicine man from Minnesota who lived in Helena, Montana for many years until his death in 1994, once was asked why star quilts are so important. He replied, "They represent the Sacred Circle, and even most Indians have forgotten that."

Indians' belief that objects can be sacred is one which many Europeans used to substantiate their insistence that these natives were pagan peoples. These Europeans, who came here partly for the freedom to worship as they saw fit, saw no need to accord Indians that same freedom. Another thing which Europeans believed indicated the pagan nature of Indians was that Indians worshiped many gods. This is not true. Indians believe in one Creator, sometimes called Wakan-Tanka, the Great Mysterious One, or the Great Spirit, who moves in all living things. Therefore, Indians treat all living things with reverence and respect. The Oglala Sioux have a specific phrase to denote this familial relationship, "mitakuye oyasin," meaning "all my relations," which includes every living thing. The Sun Dance, which has been believed by whites to be the worship of the sun, is in truth a form of prayer. The Oglala words "wiwanyag wachipi," mean "dance looking at the sun." The Sun Dance is among the most vital of the rites held by Plains Indians today. The Sioux, for example, have held it annually during the Moon of Fattening in June or the Moon of Cherries Blackening in July. This prayer dance is another way to thank the Creator for good fortune bestowed.

Indians believe that objects have power. The power found in objects, which comes from an understanding of the object's meaning, is a gift from the Creator. Medicine shields and pipes are sacred objects. Things of nature, such as buffalo hides and rocks, are sacred and can become more sacred through their use with drums, shields, or medicine bundles. Sacred objects are believed to have power, which Eddie Barbeau says comes from the Creator, through the maker to the object.

✳

Women and Craft-making

The importance to Indian women of craft-making in general, and quilting in particular, cannot be overstated. A woman's place in society, and her influence, have been directly related to her ability to contribute to her family's economic well-being.

Among Plains Indians, women have always served an important role in the culture and have been held in high esteem from their birth. Traditionally, a young woman's first "isnati" (menstrual period) was treated as a sacred event because it signalled her ability to bear children. In the old days, the young woman was taken to dwell alone in a small tepee for four days, during which an older woman would instruct her about the things she ought to know.

Fort Peck Reservation, maker unknown, give-away quilt, satin

Fort Peck Reservation, maker unknown, give-away quilt, satin

Fort Peck Reservation, made by Christine Owens, give-away quilt

Fort Peck Reservation, made by Christine Owens, give-away quilt

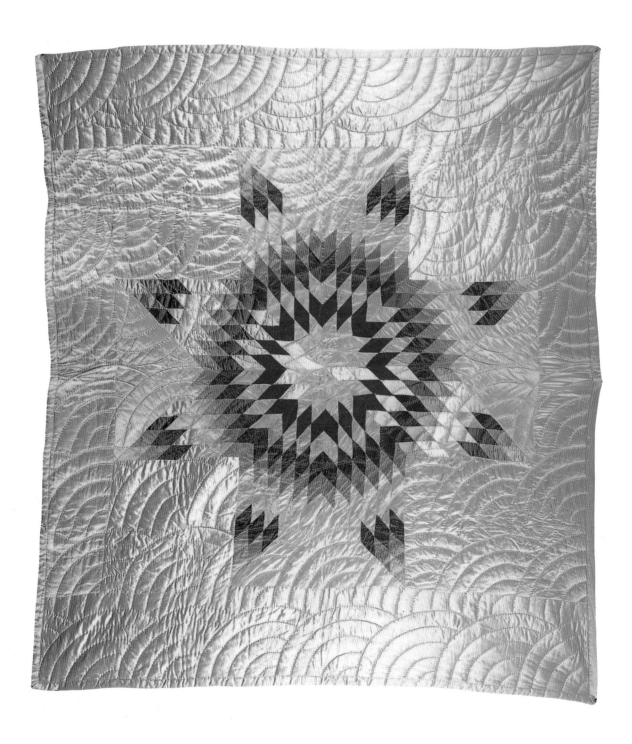

Fort Peck Reservation, made by Loretta Bear Cub, give-away quilt, satin

Fort Peck Reservation, maker unknown, give-away quilt, satin

Made by Linda Parker for Max's testing.

The older woman, being the only person allowed to go near the young girl, would bring her all the things she needed. Also, the older woman was expected to be good and pure because her virtues were considered to be transferred to the young woman. On the fourth day of the "isnati," a ritual was performed, followed by a feast and give-away held in honor of the young woman. Menstruation was thought to have a strange power, which in some cases could bring harm to the young woman or to others. Women were considered to have a strong influence during their period, and could actually take away the power of a medicine man. They were expected to stay away from men's medicine bags and from ceremonies during this time.

Due to the strong influence of tribal values, a young woman always knew what was expected of her. A virtuous, physically attractive woman, thrifty and proficient at feminine tasks, was considered ideal. Young women who knew how to prepare hides and cook well were recognized as potentially good wives. Their virtue was also connected to their skills, because girls who were kept at home learning skills avoided getting into trouble. A virtuous girl would make a good wife, as her skills could create a worthy tepee which other tribal members would desire to enter. Such a girl would attract a fine young man from one of the best families, who would bring many gifts and horses as her bride price, thereby bestowing honor on her family. Gifts indicated the ability of the man to support the woman, and reflected the esteem in which the girl was held. On the other hand, a foolish woman who chose not to learn the things considered appropriate for her to know could become an outcast.

In Plains Indian culture it was important for a woman to become accomplished at a specific craft, because through trading her wares she could increase the wealth and honor of her family and add to her own value in society. An industrious and talented woman could increase her husband's fortunes through payment received for her work. Since the man's position depended on his ability to give away large amounts of goods, the woman's contribution was vital to his status and prestige. Also, through her craft-making a woman could maintain a certain amount of power over men's behavior by controlling the goods he needed. Although in some tribes certain goods were made by men, generally it was the women who produced the goods which men sold, traded or gave away. Women used buffalo, deer and elk hides to make such items as clothing, tepees, containers and ropes.

Specialization in a craft was maintained in two ways: by teachers being selective about how many people they taught, and by cultural rituals essential to do the work without risk. The techniques and rituals performed to do the work properly were kept secret in order to protect the knowledge of the crafts. A woman had to express a sincere, internal desire to learn a specific craft, and persuade the teacher that she was worthy of being taught. Instructors were always compensated for their expertise. Only when the instructor believed there was ample need for work in the village would she agree to teach. When the teacher considered her student adept in a craft, she would help her set out on her own by sending business to her. A woman who was poor might ask to be taught a craft in order to increase her own and her family's wealth and status. She would also have the opportunity to become a member of a select craft society.

Although craft-making was taught to those who presented themselves as worthy students in order to pass on techniques and rituals to a new generation, a teacher also received some payment from her student for training. For example, a young Mandan woman helping her mother make clay pots would prepare a simple feast to which other females of the household were invited. By doing this she received the right to continue helping make pots, and to make her own after her mother died. A student's payment was usually insignificant in comparison to the value of the goods. The small payment simply expressed the young woman's respect for her teacher and for the values of her society.

33

Fort Peck Reservation, maker unknown, give-away quilt

Fort Peck Reservation, maker unknown, give-away quilt

Fort Peck Reservation, maker unknown, give-away quilt

Original design made by Linda Parker

Billings, Montana, made by Jerry Belgarde, Tee-pee star

In some instances, sacred power was associated with craft production. Dreams often indicated supernatural sanction to participate in craft work. The male or female who most closely approximated the ideals of virtue and proficiency was assumed to have received supernatural assistance. In other situations, special ceremonies or status were required for participation in craft work. For example, among the Assiniboine, the tanning of white buffalo hides was done by the wives of chiefs. Among the Dakota, the tanner was required to be a virgin.

✳

The Star Quilter

In the late 19th century, when the Sioux first settled on reservations, buffalo became scarce and textiles imported by traders began to be used by women craft- makers. The buffalo had been fundamentally important to Plains Indians because it offered almost everything needed for their daily life. Its meat was eaten and its hide was tanned for clothing, robes and tepees. Its bones were used for spoons, needles, combs, backscratchers, sleds, carved toys, ornaments, necklaces, beads and breastplates. It is intriguing that Indian women, through their own ingenuity, were able to substitute items made from textiles for items made from the buffalo, creating new "traditions" with these new materials.

The Ladies Aid Society of the Dakota Presbyterian Church is believed to be responsible for the introduction of quilt making on the various Indian reservations. Star quilts became the most popular design. Fan quilting was the most commonly accepted style of quilting, followed by shell quilting, another popular style. The Ladies Aid Society may have introduced the style of fan quilting, which was also used by the Baptists in Texas. The fan quilting style was adopted by Indians, because of its circular shape and not ease of quilting. Not all of the Plains Indians were initially receptive to the new craft brought by the Ladies Aid. Some of the tribes who were, and who are still recognized for their star quilt making are the Assiniboine, Sioux, Gros Ventre, Mandan, Hidatsa, Cree and Chippewa.

Interest in Plains Indian art and culture among whites has grown during the last decade, although there continues to be a lack of recognition given the artists, especially the women. Most Plains Indian tribes, however, regard the Star Quilt Maker in high esteem, and Star Quilt Makers take great pride in the individuality of their work. For example, Almira Jackson, a highly respected quilter, tends to use diamonds out to the edges of her quilts instead of confining them to the central pattern. Jerry Belgarde places interesting designs in her borders and sometimes adds them to the backs of her quilts, in addition to creating distinctive stars. Both Almira and Jerry have made many star quilts, possibly hundreds and thus are recognized Star Quilt Makers. In contrast, a woman who has just made a few basic give-away quilts is not given the status of Star Quilt Maker. For that status, quantity, as well as quality, is essential.

Star Quilt Makers rarely make the same quilt twice and copy-catting is frowned upon. Color changes and fabric or design alterations allow each quilt to be unique. Every quilter is encouraged to explore her own creativity. A traditional star quilt is made with many solid colors of cotton diamonds on a white or light-colored background. Satin fabric is a common substitute. Designs are occasionally used within the star, such as eagles, tepees, horses or pipes, but they are exceptions usually made for a special ceremony or person. Four women may make tepee designs within the eight points of a star, yet each tepee will be different. Reds, oranges, blues and purples may be used in ten quilts, yet each quilt will have a different arrangement of colors. In this way the star quilter's imagination transcends the limited availability of materials.

Fort Peck Reservation, maker unknown, give-away quilt. Presented to Jack Kober in 1981 in honor of his marriage.

Fort Peck Reservation, maker unknown, give-away quilt. Presented to Jack Kober in 1983 at Eastern "B" Division basketball tournament in Miles City, by Poplar cheerleader, member of Boyd Family Singers and sister of Debra Boyd, superintendent's secretary.

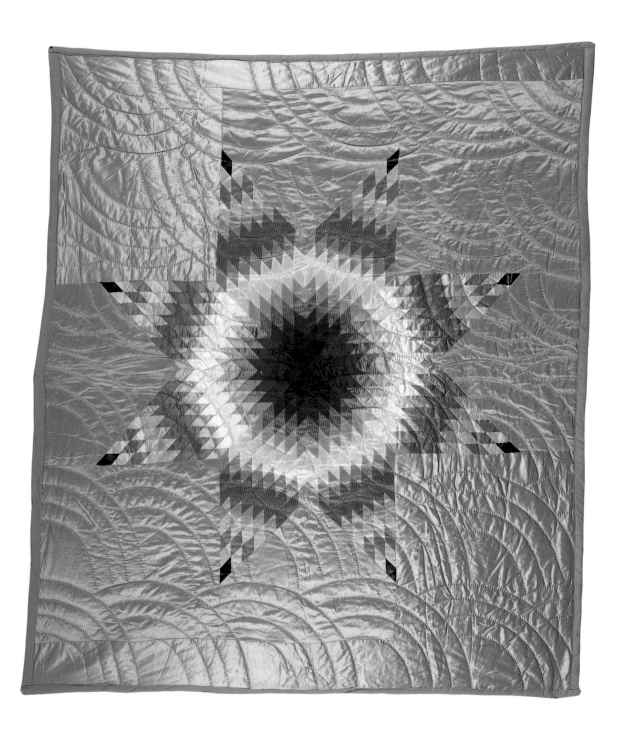

Fort Peck Reservation, maker unknown, give-away quilt, satin. Presented to Jack Kober in 1984 by the Fort Peck Tribal Council at the time of his retirement, honoring his eight years as superintendent of schools.

Fort Peck Reservation, made by Almira Jackson, give-away quilt. Presented to Linda Parker.

Fort Peck Reservation, maker unknown

The Indian quilting experience is often different from that of whites, as Indian quilters have little access to quilting supply stores. For this reason diamonds are cut from whatever material is available and it's rare that a quilter goes out to buy the exact fabric needed to complete a quilt. Rather, friends and relatives living in other places always try to bring fabric for their quilting friends when visiting. Also, most Indian quilters know how to make diamond templates just by folding a piece of paper and cutting along one edge. The diamond template is perfect, and any size one wants can be made with no measuring devices involved.

Indians tend to use brighter, bolder colors than white quilters and different colors represent different things, to each tribe. Colors may represent the four directions traveled by the four winds, the four powers of the universe, or the four seasons. Black Elk once said he saw the morning star change colors—(from red to blue, to yellow and then finally white, and that in them he saw the four ages). These colors are commonly found in various combinations within Indian star quilts. Quilts made in red, white and blue, or military quilts, honor men and women entering the military or returning from duty. The colors of other quilts may have no special significance, but simply may be the colors that a woman has on hand or happens to like. Some women dream quilt colors and designs. Such dreams are an important part of life, a gift from the Creator. Almira Jackson has said she sometimes dreams about the quilts she creates. She says that some of the quilt color combinations may seem unusual, but outdoors, you may see the colors growing next to each other.

Another unique feature of Indian star quilts is that they are not available to the general public. Even though a Star Quilt Maker can completely finish a quilt in 24 hours they are seldom offered for sale off the reservations, because of the high demand for quilts within the culture. Also, Star Quilt Makers are dedicated to sharing their work and spreading their sense of love and friendship with every quilt they give away. The quilter rarely receives a star quilt, nor will you find one in her own home. She simply has too many reasons to sell or give them away. Making your own thus becomes a good way to appreciate star quilts and the skill of the quilters who create them.

The next portion of this book will teach you the basics of making star quilts. After you have made a few, your ability to be creative with them will flourish. This book is meant to share with you the unlimited potential of star quilts. The full quilt diagrams are provided for you to copy, color or cut apart to create your own variations. Star quilts are about possibilities. The combinations of colors and connections are endless. The star can be simple or complex, bright or muted, bold or subtle. You can make these quilts forever and never have two the same. Have fun, explore, trust your intuition, and enjoy the process.

My wish is that you find great satisfaction and joy in the making and giving of star quilts. In this way you honor the traditions of the Indian women quilters whose lives exemplify sharing and giving. Each quilt is a gift of warmth, love and spirit.

Fort Peck Reservation, made by Almira Jackson, give-away quilt, lamé

Maker unknown, Seven Sisters

Fort Peck Reservation, maker unknown, End of the Trail, give-away quilt

Fort Peck Reservation, maker unknown, War Bonnet, give-away quilt

Fort Peck Reservation, maker unknown, give-away quilt

Fort Peck Reservation, maker unknown, give-away quilt

Fort Peck Reservation, made by Almira Jackson, give-away quilt, satin

Fort Peck Reservation, made by Betty Martell, give-away quilt, satin

Fort Peck Reservation, maker unknown, give-away quilt

Original design made by Linda Parker

Fort Peck Reservation, maker unknown, give-away quilt

Basic Instructions

✳

Supplies:

Scissors
Iron
Straight pins
Safety pins
Plastic for templates
Water soluble pens
24" transparent quilting ruler
Thread
Quilt frame (optional); directions for an
    Indian-style frame are included
Rotary cutter (optional)
Mat (optional)

Tips:

ALWAYS prewash fabric and press before
using!

Damp fabric that you have no time to iron
can be frozen in a plastic bag to avoid
mildew (thaw for several hours before
ironing).

Yardage based on 45" width.

Template includes ¼" seam allowances.

Most quilters prefer 100 percent cotton
fabric.

The term "press," unless otherwise specified,
means press seam to one side.

Pinning is mentioned only when it is essential. Feel free to pin more often according to
your comfort level.

Cut off the selvage. Despite what it indi-
cates, it is rarely a straight edge.

For silk, satin, or lamè, use nonwoven,
fusible interfacing on the back.

With polished cottons, it's important to
stack and use the cut pieces same-side-up.

If you must stop sewing for a length of time,
unused diamonds can be stored in a Ziploc
bag to keep the edges from fraying.

Tips of seam ripper or small scissors help
rotate fabric to align the right angles (See
Jami's Star, 3d).

TEMPLATES: Trace paper diamond onto
rigid plastic (Schwann's one-gallon ice
cream container lids work well).

Cutting Diamonds:

For a point to be constructed correctly, it is
essential that all diamonds be exactly the
same size. Placing the edge of the template
directly on the lines when marking fabric
eliminates the potential for error. Placing the
template above or beside the lines when
marking fabric may cause pieces to be off by
as much as $\frac{1}{16}$". This becomes a tragic error
when multiplied by dozens of diamonds.

Fold selvages together lengthwise; press.
Using your quilting ruler, draw a line at the
bottom of the folded fabric as a starting
point. Then mark off rows with your quilting
ruler as follows:

a   Lay one side of the diamond template
    exactly on the line at each end, and mark
    fabric on the side opposite the line. This
    is the width of the row. Using ruler,
    connect the marks.

b   Continue marking off rows up from the
    raw edge in the same manner.

c   Repeat this process until enough lines are
    drawn for the number of diamonds
    needed.

d Now, using the template, mark off a series of diamonds in each row making sure the edge of the template is placed directly on the preceding line. Repeat this step within each row, always laying diamond in the same direction.

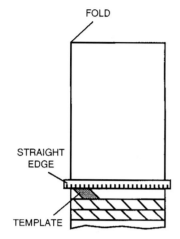

Fig XX - Cutting directions

e Finally, cut diamonds.

Cutting triangles:

Measuring one side of a point always gives the accurate beginning measurement for cutting background squares and triangles. When measuring points, check several; use the largest measurement; then add ½" to 1", as directed, to allow for seam allowances.

In the Fast Star, and designs using the Fast Star, it is always essential to cut the square for triangles 1½" larger than the point or diamond. Even though it appears too large, this size is necessary for the horizontal point to fit.

Changing Quilt Designs:

You may want to use your own color combinations, as well as rearranging diamonds and points. Each star design has a designated number of points. Once you know the number of diamonds in a point, simply multiply the number of diamonds in one point by the total number of points. Adding or subtracting a color changes the fabric yardage calculated for a pattjern. Diagrams for coloring have been provided for each quilt design; feel free to make as many copies as you wish.

The following example is for a Lone Star with eight 3½" diamonds across; finished size is 90" x 108".

To compute the number of diamonds needed for a quilt, count diamonds on one side of a point, then square that number (i.e., 8 diamonds x 8 diamonds = 64 diamonds per point). Then multiply by the number of points: 64 diamonds x 8 points = 512 diamonds for a quilt.

To compute the number of diamonds of any color in the point, count diamonds of that color in one point and multiply by 8. If making a quilt with several small points in a large point (one eighth section) count the number of diamonds in the large point. For example:

Light blue: 24 x 8 = 192

Dark blue: 6 x 8 = 48

Gray: 14 x 8 = 112

Dark gray = 20 x 8 = 160

   TOTAL = 512

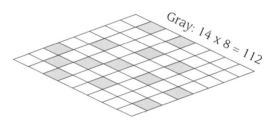

How much fabric is needed?

Now that you know the number of diamonds of each color in the quilt of your choice, you need to know how much fabric to use. Remember, all instructions are based on 45" width fabric.

Diamond Size	Diamonds Per Row	Fabric
3½"	10	2½"
2½"	14	2"
2"	20	1½"

Next, for each color, divide the total number of diamonds needed by the number of diamonds per row to arrive at the total number of rows you need to make; then multiply the number of rows by the fabric per row to arrive at the fabric requirement for that color. For example, in the above chart, 192 light blue diamonds are required. Divide 192 by 10 = 19.2 rows. Always round the number up, (here to 20). 20 rows X 2½" equals 50", or approximately 1½ yards.

The six background squares needed for this example are 24½", so only one square can be cut per width of fabric (24½" + 24½"= 49"; fabric is only 45" wide). When cutting the background squares cut along the selvage side of the fabric instead of across the width; the border strips can be cut out of the remaining length so they won't need to be pieced.

$$24½" \times 6 = 147"$$

Divide 147" by 36" for number of yards needed, which is 4 yards, 3". (45"- 24½" = 20½"; this excess fabric can be used for at least four 5" border strips.

Buying at least 3 yards of each color of fabric used in the border will ensure that border strips do not have to be pieced. Yardage given in directions does not include enough fabric to cut full length border strips without piecing.

Border Construction:

All quilts in this book have a star center and a suggested finished size. Once the star is constructed and the background pieces added, the completed star center varies in size from 44" to 65". To complete the quilt top in the suggested finished size, generally three or more border strips are added. Subtracting the measurements of the star center from the suggested finished size (plus seam allowances) gives you the number of inches needed for the border.

For example, the Fast Star's suggested finished size is 81" x 96"; its star center is approximately 44" square. To compute the widths of the border strips, complete the following:

> Subtract the star center size from the finished size; to use three border strips on each side, add 3" to each sum (for the ¼" seam allowances on each side of each of the three strips).

81	x	96
-44		-44
37+3=40		52+3=55

Divide 40 by 6 (3 strips on each side) to arrive at 6⅔" for the side strips; divide 55 by 6 to arrive at 9⅙" for the top and bottom strips. Since all sizes are approximate, you can round up or down to arrive at easily measureable sizes. In other words, when cutting the side strips, four can be 6½" and 2 can be 7"— or you can just make them all 6½" and your finished width will be 80" instead of 81". When cutting the top and bottom strips, four can be 9" and 2 can be 9½" —or you can just make them all 9" and your finished length will be 95" instead of 96". If the quilt you are making has four border strips, you will add 4" to the sums in the above computation, and you will divide by 8 rather than 6. If the quilt has only two border strips, you will add 2" to the above and you will divide by 4.

The length of each pair of strips to be cut will increase consecutively. Always measuring each side as you go will eliminate potential error in the lengths, although it doesn't hurt to add an extra ½". Excess fabric can always be trimmed; not enough requires tedious piecing.

Cut two strips of border material 6½" x 44"; cut two more strips, 9" x 57" (57" equals 44" plus 13", which is the width of the two previous strips). Sew the two 6½" x 44" strips to the sides. Press. Then sew the 9" x 57" strips to the top and bottom. Press.

For the second border strip cut two strips 6½" x 57", and two strips 9" x 70" (57" plus 13"). Sew the 6½" x 57" strips to the sides. Press. Then sew the 9" x 70" strips to the top and bottom. Press.

For the third border strip cut two strips 6½" x 70" and two strips 9" x 83" (70" plus 13"). Sew the 6½" x 70" strips to the sides. Press. Then sew the 9" x 83" strips to the top and bottom. Press.

See diagram on next page.

Border Construction

Quilt Completion

a Cut the six yards of fabric for the back into two, three-yard pieces. Sew the long edges together to make the 90" x 108" back. If your quilt is smaller in size, simply trim accordingly.

b A quilt frame can be made using four 1"x 4"s, two 8' and two 10' boards, which need to be wrapped in strips of old jeans or some similarly heavy fabric. Four 3" C-clamps are needed for the corners. Four chairs, T.V. trays or sawhorses may be used to set the boards on.

2x2 trans basic instructions/frame structure

c Using safety pins, pin the quilt back to the ends of the two short boards; stretch boards with pinned fabric to opposite ends of the long boards and clamp. Now place batting on top of quilt back and stretch it out relatively tight. Place quilt top on the batting; lightly pin the four corners. Starting with the ends on the short boards, pin the batting to the back, leaving the pins in the back for now. After both ends are pinned begin removing the pins from the back and stretching the quilt top, back and batting out together, replacing pins as you go.

After both ends are complete, pin sides. Leave all the pins open until you are ready to begin rolling the quilt, then just close the end pins; the side pins will be removed as you roll.

Quilt as desired, rolling when needed.

d   Binding can be made from cutting or
    tearing four strips 3" wide, the length
    you need for the quilt. Sew the top side
    first on the sewing machine; trim excess
    batting and fabric, then sew the back
    side by hand.

Fort Peck Reservation, made by Almira Jackson, give-away quilt

Fort Peck Reservation, maker unknown, give-away quilt

Fort Peck Reservation, made by Almira Jackson, give-away quilt

Fort Peck Reservation, maker unknown, give-away quilt

Fort Peck Reservation, maker unknown, Flying Swallows, give-away quilt

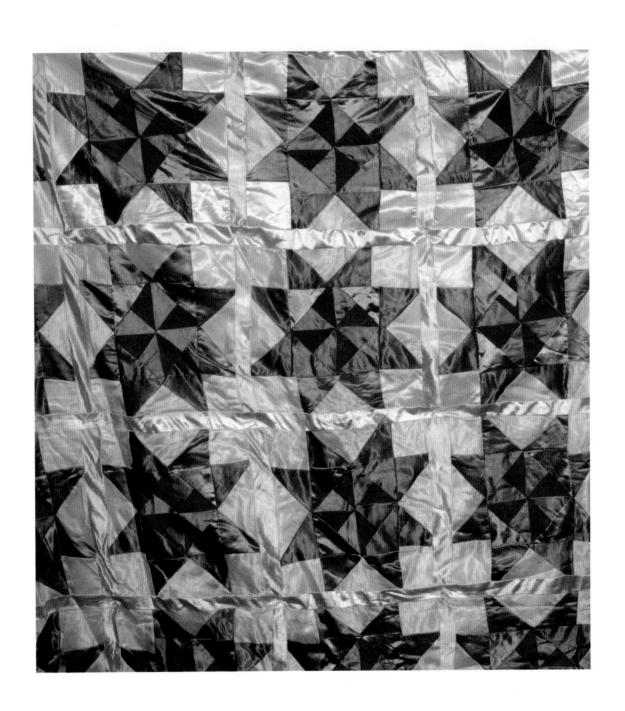

Havre, Montana, maker unknown, give-away quilt

Lone Star

Made by Linda Parker for Jeanne Eder

Lone Star

✳

The Lone Star is probably the most commonly used star quilt design on Montana reservations and it is often called a "star blanket." In the Anglo-American quilting community it is also known as the Texas Lone Star or the Star of Bethlehem. The Lone Star is a popular quilt for a give-away since a star quilter can complete the top in about six hours, depending on its size.

The Lone Star's beauty is in its radiating, repetitive sunburst design. Indian quilting history tells us that this quilt design has been made primarily using solid color diamonds with a white or light background since at least the 1930s. Its popularity within Indian cultures stems from its obvious resemblance to the sacred circle formerly painted on buffalo robes, and to the Morning Star. It often starts with eight center diamonds forming a circle, followed by concentric circles of different colors. The diamond colors can be rearranged for an almost limitless variety of strikingly different designs within the star. The use of half-diamonds allows exquisite detail in the picture presented within the star. This adds a great deal to the fun and satisfaction of creating something which is uniquely your own.

To change the size of the quilt, simply add or subtract rows of diamonds. A simple rule of thumb is to use five 3½" diamonds across for a single, six for a double, seven for a queen, and eight for a king. As an alternative, you may also change the size of the diamonds or the width of the border strips.

✳

Finished size: 90" X 108"
Fabric:
A: Teal: 2 yards
B: Light blue: 3¾ yards
C: Blue print: 2¼ yards
D: Turquoise: 1¾ yards
Quilt back: 6 yards color of choice
Binding: excess of color A, B or C

1 **Read through these directions** before starting, then see basic instructions for cutting diamonds and squares. It is essential to cut the triangles 1" larger than the point. When constructing the quilt top, pin/sew right sides together.

2 **Point Construction:**
2a Using diamond template size 3½",
Cut 120 diamonds Color A
Cut 80 diamonds Color B
Cut 128 diamonds color C
Cut 64 diamonds color D

The diagrams show the precise order in which to sew the diamonds into rows. Remember to keep tops at the top when sewing rows together, as it is easy to inadvertently reverse one.

2b Sew the first row of diamonds from the top to the bottom. Press.

2c Sew the second row of diamonds from the top to the bottom. Press. Pin the second row to the first row at diamond intersections, then sew. Press.

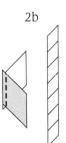
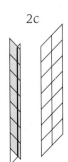

2b   2c

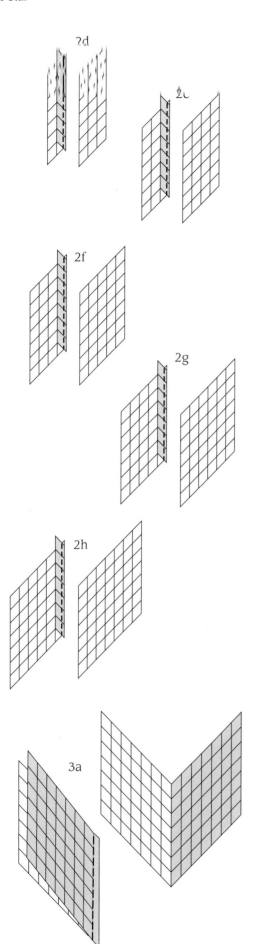

2d Sew the third row as above. Press. Pin the third row to the second row at diamond intersections then sew. Press.

2e Sew the fourth row as above. Press. Pin fourth row to the third row at diamond intersections, then sew. Press.

2f Sew the fifth row as above. Press. Pin the fifth row to the fourth row at diamond intersections, then sew. Press.

2g Sew the sixth row as above. Press. Pin the sixth row to the fifth row at diamond intersections, then sew. Press.

2h Sew the seventh row as above. Press. Pin the seventh row to the sixth row at diamond inter-sections, then sew. Press.

2i Repeat 2b through 2h seven times.

Row	1	2	3	4	5	6	7
	A	C	D	C	D	B	A
	C	B	A	B	C	A	B
	D	A	A	C	A	C	D
	C	B	C	A	C	B	C
	D	C	A	C	A	A	D
	B	A	C	B	A	B	C
	A	B	D	C	D	C	A

3   Sewing Star Points:

3a Pin two points to each other at diamond intersec-tions, then sew. Press. Repeat 3 times.

3b Pin two pairs of points to each other at diamond intersections, then sew. Press. Repeat.

3c Pin the two halves to each other at diamond intersections, then sew. You may prefer to sew starting from the center, out. Press.

4   Background Construction:

4a Measure one side of a point, add 1". Cut six squares this size of color B. Fold two squares diagonally into two equal triangles. Press. Cut along the fold line.

4b Pin a color B triangle to the point, then sew, with the triangle on the top, from A to B. Leaving needle in at B, lift presser foot, clip, then rotate. Use seam ripper or tips of small scissors to help turn the fabric. Continue sewing from B to C. Triangle fabric will extend slightly beyond the point. Press. Sew the remaining triangles, skipping every other space between points. Press.

4c Sew the four background squares into the corners in the same manner.

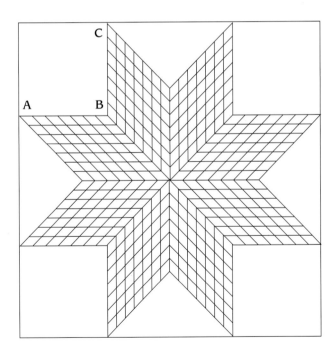

5   Border, quilting and binding directions are included in the basic instructions. Note: this quilt uses four border strips on each side rather than three.

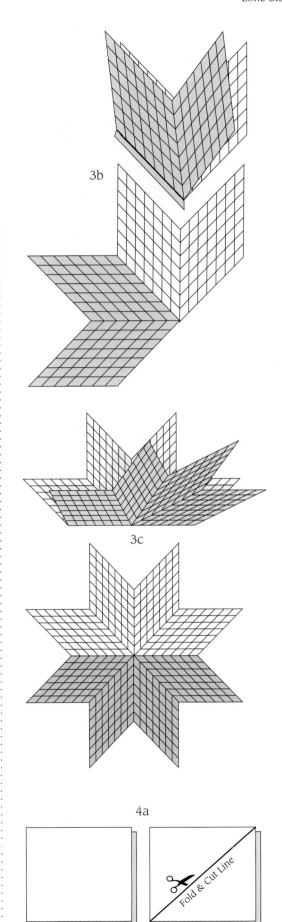

Lone Star Variations

Made by Linda Parker

Made by Linda Parker for Max's Testing. Marj Bourne photo

Lone Star

Fast Star

Made by Linda Parker

Fast Star

*

The Fast Star is the only uniquely Indian design with directions included in Montana Star Quilts. The Fast Star is one of the most beautiful star quilt designs I have seen; the versatility and adaptability of its points allow this pattern to be as intricate or as simple as you wish. Jerry Belgarde says she saw a Fast Star at a friend's house and liked it so much she went right home and made one. "The design has just always been there," Jerry explained. "I've seen it at a lot of give-aways, and never anywhere else."

Since it has just 96 diamonds, an experienced star quilter needs only three or four hours to cut and completely sew the top. Considering the number of star quilts a quilter might be asked to make in any given year for give-aways, its name is self-explanatory.

The Fast Star design may be an adaptation of the Flying Swallows since it uses a different arrangement of the same number of points and triangles. Varying the number of diamonds and their arrangement in each point has stunning effects. (See Jerry's Feather quilt on page 6 which has nine diamonds per point, and her Eagle Star on page 82, where the center points have been replaced with the eagle.)

Because it is the foundation for so many other patterns, becoming adept with the Fast Star will simplify the construction of other quilts in this book.

*

Finished size: 81" X 96"
Fabric:
A: Red solid: 3⅙ yards
B: Black print: 2⅓ yards
C: Gray solid: 2 yards
D: Black solid: 1½ yards
Quilt back: 6 yards color of choice
Binding: 1 yard color of choice

1 **Read through these directions** before starting; then see basic instructions for cutting diamonds and squares. It is essential to cut the triangles 1½" larger than the point. When constructing the quilt top, pin/sew right sides together.

2 **Small Point Construction**
2a Using diamond template size 3½",
   Cut 48 diamonds Color A
   Cut 48 diamonds Color B

2b Sew diamonds, colors A & B together to make the first row of two diamonds. Repeat 47 times. Press half with seams toward color A and half with seams toward color B.

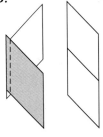

2c Sew two rows of diamonds together with color A at both points. Repeat 23 times. Press.

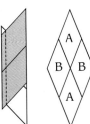

3a

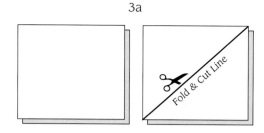

3 Large Point Construction

Again, it is essential to always cut the triangles 1½" larger than the point. Even though they appear too large, this size is necessary for the horizontal point to fit. Also, measuring one side of a point, then adding 1½" always gives the accurate size of the square, which here should be 8".

3a Cut sixteen 8" squares of color C. Fold each square diagonally into two equal triangles. Press. Cut along the fold line.

3b Sew one short side of a triangle to a point from step 2c. Do not line up the edges evenly; rather, the bottom of the triangle extends only ¼", with the excess extending over the top of the small point. DO NOT TRIM any excess fabric yet. Press seams away from point. Repeat 15 times.

3c Sew a second triangle to the opposite side of the point. Again, the bottom of the triangle extends only ¼" with the excess extending over the top of the point. DO NOT TRIM any excess fabric yet. Press seams away from point. Repeat 15 times.

3d Sew another point from step 2c sideways into the V completed in 3c. Pin at B then sew from A to B. Leaving needle in at B, lift presser foot, clip, then rotate. Continue sewing from B to C. Now trim excess triangle fabric. Press seams toward the V. Repeat 7 times.

3e Sew another 3c piece to a completed 3d piece. Pin at B then sew from A to B. Leaving needle in at B, lift presser foot, clip, then rotate. Continue sewing from B to C. Now trim excess triangle fabric. Press seams toward the V. Repeat 7 times.

3b

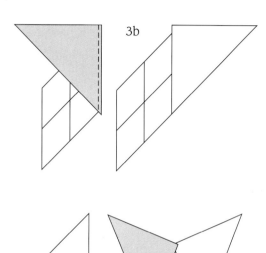

3c

3d

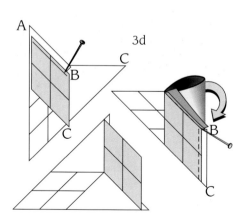

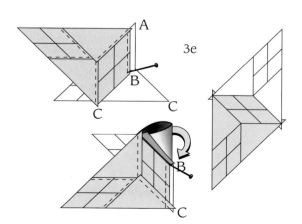

3e

4 Sewing Star Points

4a Pin two large points to each other, making sure the horizontal points touch but **do not** overlap and sides of the vertical points line up exactly, then sew. Press. Repeat 3 times.

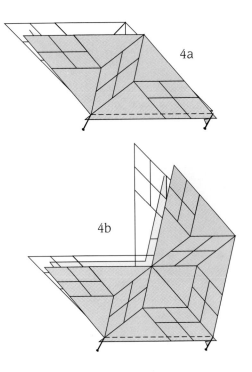

4b Pin two pairs of large points to each other, again making sure the horizontal points and the vertical points line up exactly, then sew. Press. repeat.

4c Pin the two halves to each other, again making sure the horizontal and vertical points line up exactly, then sew. you may prefer to sew starting from the center out. Press.

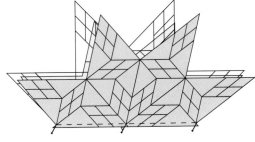

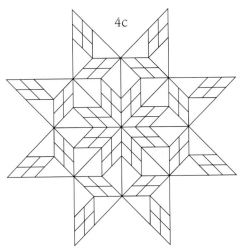

Made by Linda Parker for Max's Testing.
Marj Bourne photo

5 Background Construction

5a Measure one side of a point, add 1". Cut two squares this size of color A and four of color D. Fold each square diagonally into twoe qual triangles. Press. Cut along the fold line.

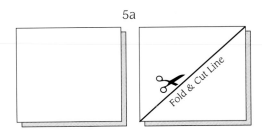

5b Pin a color D triangle to the point, then sew, with the triangle on the top, from A to B. Leaving needle in at B, lift presser foot, clip, then rotate. Continue sewing from B to C. Triangle fabric will extend slightly beyond the point. Press. Repeat 7 times.

5c Sew long sides of color A
triangles to the four corners.
Press.

6 **Border Construction**
Border quilting and binding
directions are included in the
basic instructions.

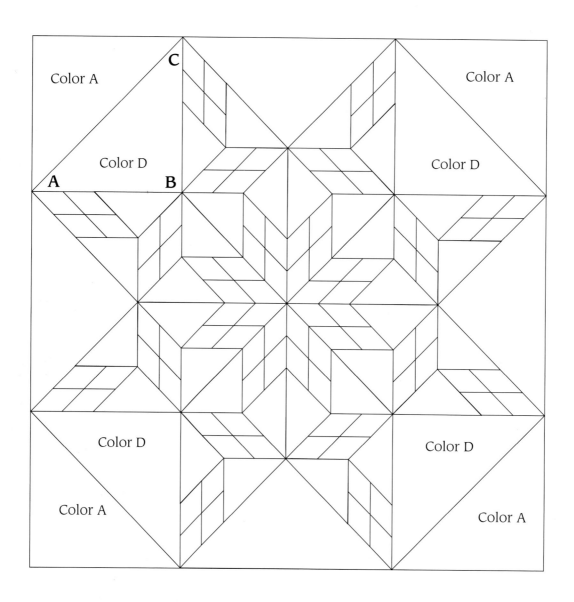

Color A

C

Color A

Color D

Color D

A

B

Color D

Color D

Color A

Color A

Fast Star Variations

Made by Linda Parker. Black and White Photography, Billings, Mont., photo

Fast Star

Jerry Belgarde's Eagle Star Quilt

Billings, Montana, original design by Jerry Belgarde, Eagle Star

Eagle Star

Eagle Star Quilt Template

Large Eagle 1

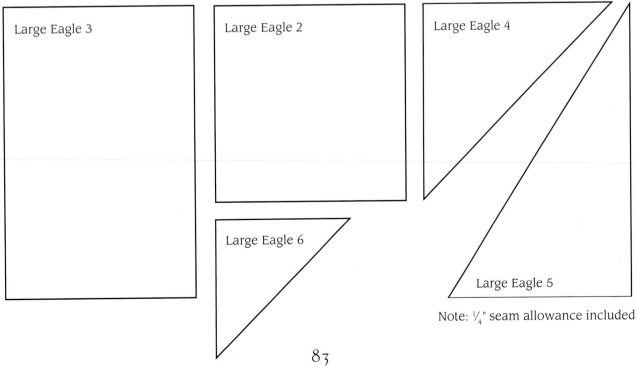

Large Eagle 3

Large Eagle 2

Large Eagle 4

Large Eagle 6

Large Eagle 5

Note: $\frac{1}{4}$" seam allowance included

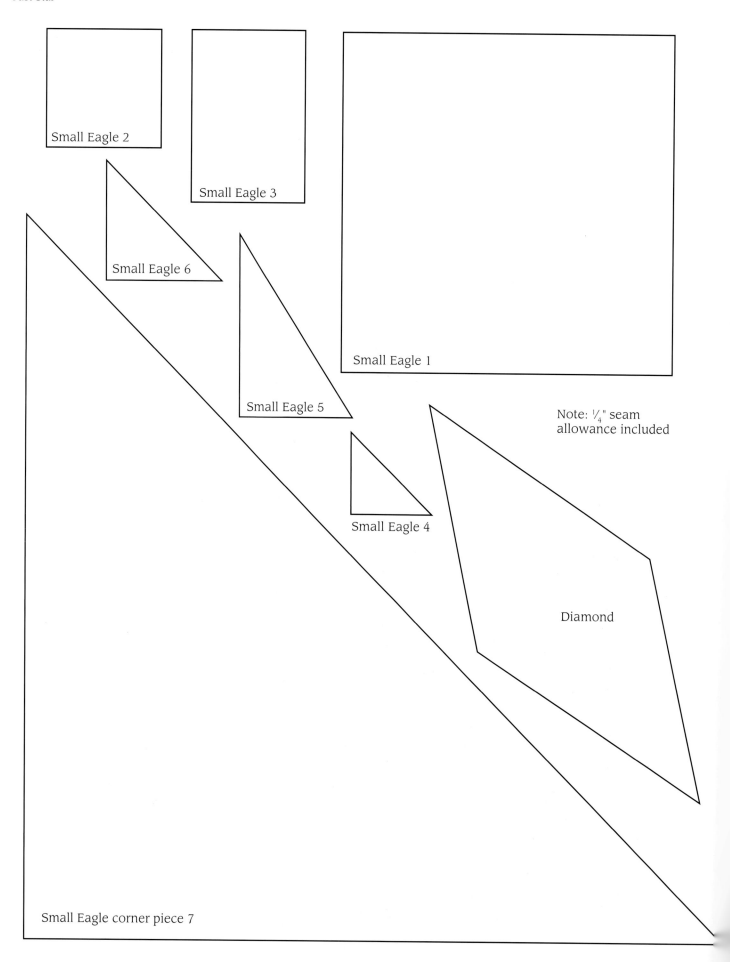

Small Eagle 2

Small Eagle 3

Small Eagle 6

Small Eagle 1

Small Eagle 5

Note: ¼" seam
allowance included

Small Eagle 4

Diamond

Small Eagle corner piece 7

Eagle Star Quilt Head Block

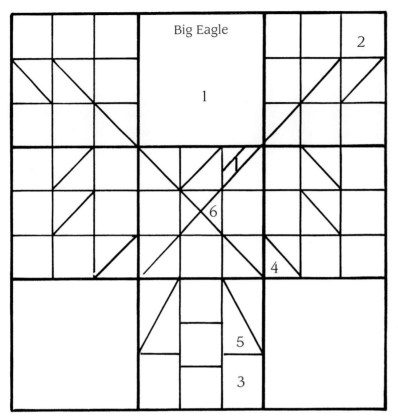

See page 82 for small eagle #7 placement.

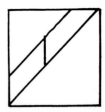

Looking to right

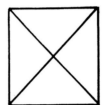

Small center block

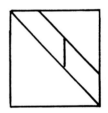

Looking to left

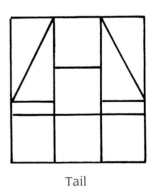

Tail

Made by Linda Parker

Jami's Star

Original design made by Linda Parker

Jami's Star

✳

Finished size: 81" X 96"

Finished Fabric:

A: Blue: 4½ yards

B: Red: 1⅔ yards

C: Yellow: ¾ yards

D: Purple: ⅓ yards

E: Orange: ½ yards

Quilt back: 6 yards color of choice

Binding: excess of color A or B

1 Read through these directions before starting, then see basic instructions for cutting diamonds. It is essential to cut the triangles 1½" larger than the point. When constructing the quilt top, pin/sew right sides together.

2 Small Point Construction

2a Using diamond template size 2½"

Cut 96 diamonds Color A

Cut 48 diamonds Color B

Cut 144 diamonds Color C

Cut 48 diamonds Color D

Cut 96 diamonds Color E

The diagrams show the precise order in which to sew the diamonds into rows. Remember to keep tops at the top when sewing rows together, as it is easy to inadvertently reverse one.

2b Sew the first row of diamonds from the top to the bottom. Press.

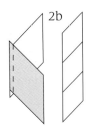

2c Sew the second row of diamonds from the top to the bottom. Press. Pin second row to first row at diamond intersections, then sew. Press.

2d Sew the third row as above. Press. Pin third row to second row at diamond intersections, then sew. Press.

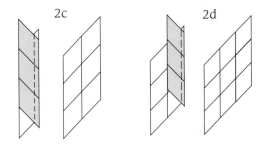

2e Repeat 2b through 2d 31 times.

2f Repeat 2b through 2d 16 times with diamonds in alternate arrangement.

Row 2b-2e			Row 2f		
1	2	3	1	2	3
B	E	C	C	E	B
E	C	A	A	C	E
C	A	D	D	A	C

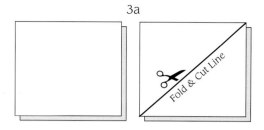

3a

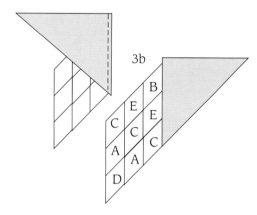

3b

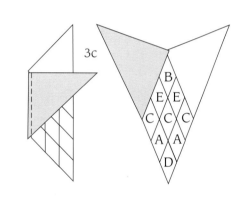

3c

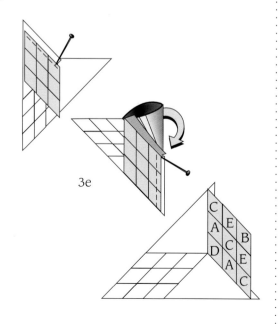

3e

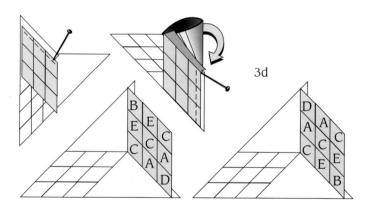

3d

3   Partial Fast Star Point Construction

3a Cut 34, 8" squares of color A. Fold each square diagonally into two equal triangles. Press. Cut along the fold line.

3b Sew one short side of a triangle to the color B tip of a point from step 2e. Do not line up the edges evenly; rather, the bottom of the triangle extends only ¼", with the excess extending over the top of the point. **DO NOT TRIM** any excess fabric yet. Press seams away from point. Repeat 23 times.

3c Sew a second triangle to the opposite side of the color B tip of the point. Again, the bottom of the triangle extends only ¼" with the excess extending over the top of the point. DO NOT TRIM any excess fabric yet. Press seams away from point. Repeat 23 times.

3d Sew a point from step 2e sideways into the V completed in 3c, with the color B tip to the left. Pin at B then sew from A to B. Leaving needle in at B, lift presser foot, clip, then rotate. Continue sewing from B to C. Now trim excess triangle fabric. Press seams toward the V. Repeat 3 times, then repeat 4 times with the color B tip to the right.

3e Sew a point from 2f sideways into the V of a 3c piece as explained in 3d with the color D side toward the center of the V. Repeat 15 times.

4 Sewing Inner Star Points

4a Sew the short side of a triangle from 3a to the left side of the horizontal point of a completed 3d piece. Do not trim any excess fabric yet. Press. Repeat 3 times.

4b Sew the short side of a triangle from 3a to the right side of the horizontal point of another completed 3d piece. Do not trim any excess fabric yet. Press. Repeat 3 times.

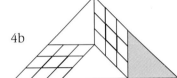

4c Pin a 4a piece and a 4b piece to each other with the 3a triangles together, making sure that the horizontal points touch but do not overlap and the sides of the vertical points line up exactly, then sew, leaving approximately ¾" of the seam open on the triangle end to facilitate fitting the outer points in step 6a. Press. Repeat 3 times.

4d Pin two pairs of large points to each other, again making sure the horizontal points and the sides of the vertical points line up exactly, then sew. Press. Repeat.

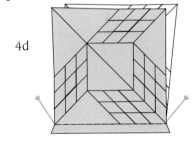

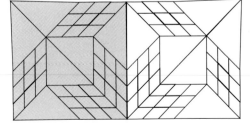

4e Pin the two halves to each other, again making sure the horizontal and vertical points line up exactly, then sew. You may prefer to sew starting from the center out. Press. Now trim excess triangle fabric so the completed square has straight edges.

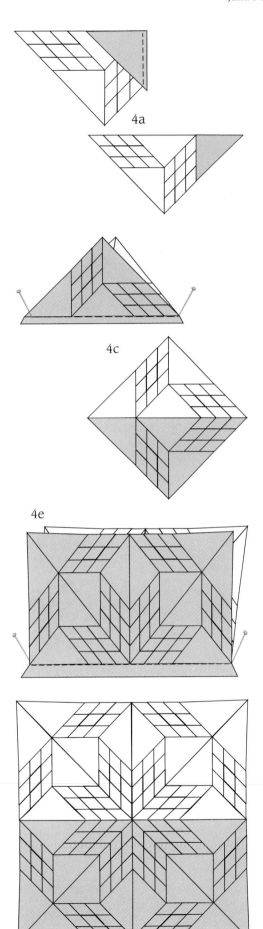

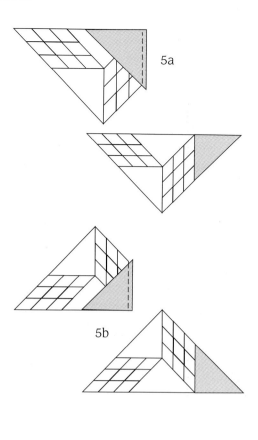

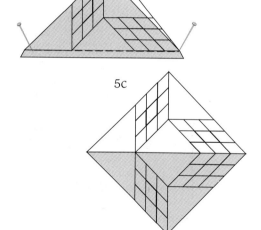

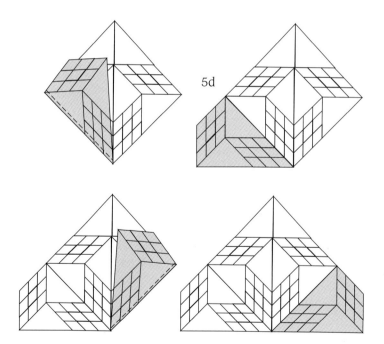

5 Sewing Outer Star Points

5a Sew the short side of a triangle from 3a to the left side of the horizontal point of a completed 3e piece. Do not trim excess fabric yet. Press. Repeat 3 times.

5b Sew the short side of a triangle from 3a to the right side of the horizontal point of another 3e piece. Do not trim excess fabric yet. Press. Repeat 3 times.

5c Pin a 5a piece and a 5b piece to each other with the 3a triangles together, making sure the horizontal points touch but do not overlap and the sides of the vertical points line up exactly, then sew. Press. Repeat 3 times.

5d Pin a 3e piece to each side of a 5c piece, making sure the horizontal points touch but do not overlap and the sides of the vertical points line up exactly, then sew. Press. Repeat 3 times.

6 Sewing Outer Points to Inner Points

6a Pin a 5d piece to one side of the square completed in 4e, making sure the sides of the vertical points line up exactly, then sew. Press. Repeat 3 times.

6b Now complete each seam left unfinished in step 4c.

6c Pin a triangle from 3a to the side of a point at the open area on a side, then sew, with the triangle on the top, from A to B. Leaving needle in at B, lift presser foot, clip, then rotate. Continue sewing from B to C. Press. Repeat. Press. Trim excess triangle fabric.

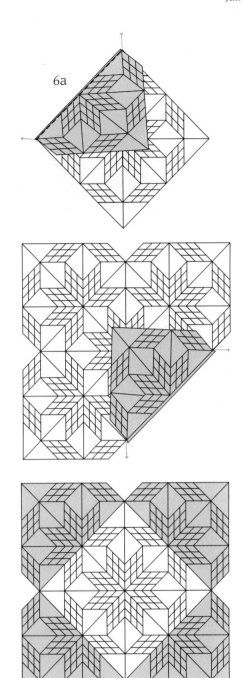

6a

6c

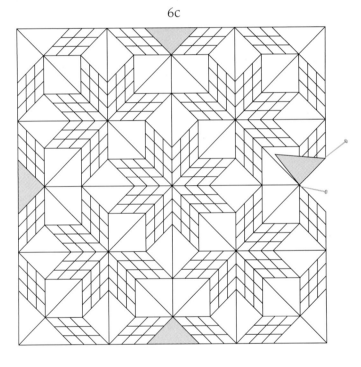

7 Border, quilting and binding directions are included in the basic instructions.

Variation of Jami's Star

Original design made by Linda Parker

Jami's Star

Jennifer's Star

Original design made by Linda Parker

Jennifer's Star

✳

Finished size: 90" X 108"

Fabric:

A: Rose: 2 yards

B: Black print: 2¾ yards

C: Light green: 4¼ yards

D: Medium Green: 2 yard

E: Dark Green: 1¾ yards

Quilt back: 6 yards color of choice

Binding: excess of color A, B or D

1   **Read through these directions** before starting, then see basic instructions for cutting diamonds and squares. It is essential to cut the triangles 1½" larger than the point. When constructing the quilt top, pin/sew right sides together.

2   **Small Point Construction**

2a Using diamond template size 3½"

    Cut 48 diamonds Color A

    Cut 96 diamonds Color B

    Cut 48 diamonds Color D

2b Sew diamonds, colors A & B together to make the first row of two diamonds. Repeat 47 times. Press seams toward color A.

2b

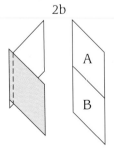

2c Sew diamonds color B & D together to make the second row of two diamonds. Repeat 47 times. Press seams toward color D.

2d) Sew the two rows of diamonds together with color A at one point and color D at the other. Repeat 47 times. Press.

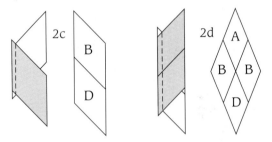

3   **Fast Star Point Construction**

Again, it is essential to always cut the triangles 1½" larger than the point. Even though they appear too large, this size is necessary for the horizontal point to fit. Also, measuring one side of a point, then adding 1½" always gives the accurate size of the square, which here should be 8".

3a Cut 16, 8" squares of color E. Fold each square diagonally into two equal triangles. Press. Cut along the fold line.

3a

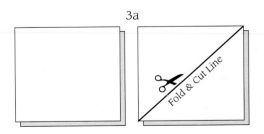

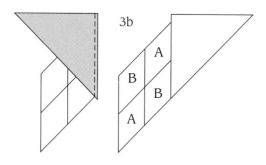

3b

3b
Sew one short side of a triangle to a point from step 2d on the end with the Color A diamond. Do not line up the edges evenly; rather, the bottom of the triangle extends only ¼" with the excess extending over the top of the small point. **DO NOT TRIM** any excess fabric yet. Press seams away from point. Repeat 15 times.

3c
Sew a second triangle to the opposite side of the point. Again, the bottom of the triangle extends only ¼" with the excess extending over the top of the point. DO NOT TRIM any excess fabric yet. Press seams away from the point. Repeat 15 times.

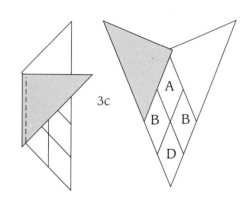

3c

3d
Sew another point from step 2d sideways into the V completed in 3c; be sure all points are placed with color A pointing the same direction. Pin at B then sew from A to B. Leaving needle in at B, lift presser foot, clip, then rotate. Continue sewing from B to C. Now trim excess triangle fabric. Press seams toward the V. Repeat 7 times.

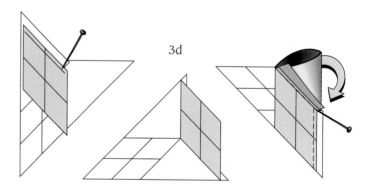

3d

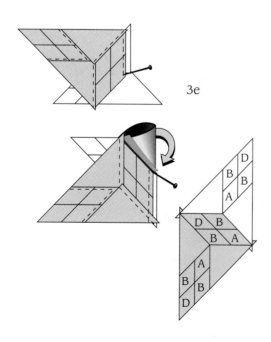

3e

3e
Sew another 3c piece to a completed 3d piece. Pin at B then sew from A to B. Leaving needle in at B, clip, then rotate. Continue sewing from B to C. Now trim excess triangle fabric. Press seams toward the V. Repeat 7 times.

4   Flying Swallow Point Construction

4a Pin two points from step 2d to each other at diamond intersection, with color D ends together, then sew. Press. Repeat 7 times.

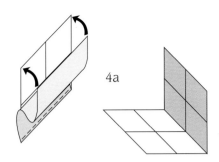

4a

4b Pin another point from step 2d to opposite side of piece from 4a at diamond intersection, with color D ends together, then sew. Press. Repeat 7 times.

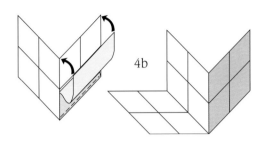

4b

4c Cut 16, 7" squares of color E. Fold each square diagonally into two equal triangles. Press. Cut along the fold line.

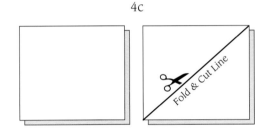

4c

4d Pin triangle from 4c to a piece from 4b in between the points, then sew, with the triangle on top, from A to B. Leaving needle in at B, lift presser foot, clip, then rotate. Continue sewing from B to C. Triangle fabric will extend slightly beyond the point. Press. Repeat 7 times.

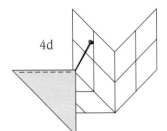 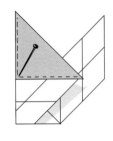

4d

4e Repeat step 4d, placing triangle in between next two points.

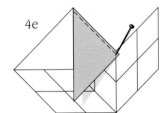 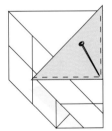

4e

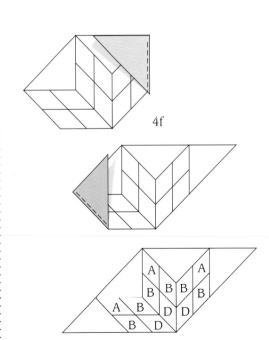

4f

4f Pin a triangle to each outside edge of the piece completed in 4e, then sew. Press. Repeat 7 times.

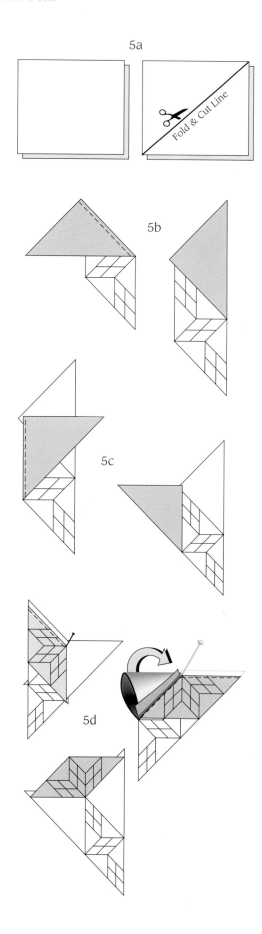

5a

5b

5c

5d

5   Background Construction

5a Cut 8, 14½" squares of color C. Fold each square diagonally into two equal triangles. Press. Cut along the fold line.

5b Sew one short side of a triangle to a point from step 3e. Do not line up the edges evenly; rather, the bottom of the triangle extends only ¼", with the excess extending over the top of the point. **DO NOT TRIM** any excess fabric yet. Press seams away from point. Repeat 7 times.

5c Sew a second triangle to the opposite side of the point. Again, the bottom of the triangle extends only ¼" with the excess extending over the top of the point. DO NOT TRIM any excess fabric yet. Press seams away from point. Repeat 7 times.

5d Sew a point from step 4f sideways into the V completed in 5c; be sure all points are placed with color D towards the center of the V. Pin at B then sew from A to B. Leaving needle in at B, lift presser foot, clip, then rotate. Continue sewing from B to C. Now trim excess triangle fabric. Press seams toward the V. Repeat 7 times.

Original design made by Linda Parker

6 Sewing Star Points

6a Pin two 5d points to each other, making sure the horizontal points touch but do not overlap and the sides of the vertical points line up exactly, then sew. Press. Repeat 3 times.

6b Pin two pairs of points from 5d to each other, again making sure the horizontal points and the sides of the vertical points line up exactly, then sew. Press. Repeat.

6c Pin the two halves to each other, again making sure the horizontal and vertical points line up exactly. Then sew the two halves. You may prefer to sew starting from the center, out. Press.

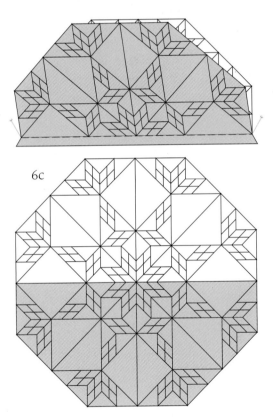

6d Cut two 19" squares color C. Fold each square diagonally into two equal triangles. Press. Cut along the fold line. Sew a triangle onto each of the four corners. Press seams same direction.

7 **Border, quilting and binding** directions are included in the basic instructions.

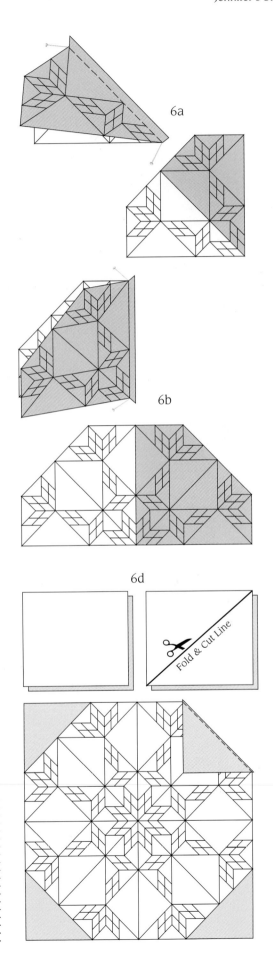

6a

6b

6d

Fold & Cut Line

Jennifer's Star Variation

Original design made by Linda Parker

Jennifer's Star

Bitterroot Star

Original design made by Linda Parker

Bitterroot Star

✳

Finished size: 90" X 108"
Fabric:
A: Blue Print: 2⅔ yards
B: Blue: 2½ yards
C: Cream: 7 yards
Quilt back: 6 yards color of choice
Binding: excess of color A

1 **Read through these directions** before starting, then see basic instructions for cutting diamonds and squares. It is essential to cut the triangles 1½" larger than the point. When constructing the quilt top, pin/sew right sides together.

2 **Small Point Construction**

2a Using diamond template size 3½"
   Cut 120 diamonds Color A
   Cut 96 diamonds Color B

2b Sew the first row of diamonds from the top to the bottom. Press.

2c Sew the second row of diamonds from the top to the bottom. Press. Pin second row to first row at diamond intersections, then sew. Press.

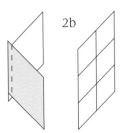

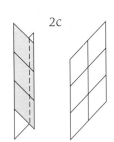

2d Sew the third row as above. Press. Pin third row to second row at diamond intersections, then sew. Press.

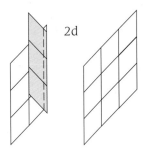

2e Repeat 2b through 2d, 23 times.

3 **Fast Star Point Construction**

3a Cut 16, 11" squares of color C. Fold each square diagonally into two equal triangles. Press. Cut along the fold line.

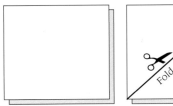
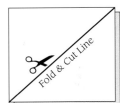

3b Sew one short side of a triangle to a point from step 2e. Do not line up the edges evenly; rather, the bottom of the triangle extends only ¼", with the excess extending over the top of the point. DO NOT TRIM any excess fabric yet. Press seams away from point. Repeat 7 times.

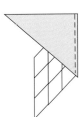
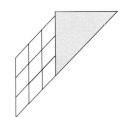

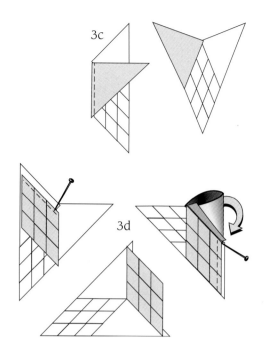

3c

3d

3c Sew a second triangle to the opposite side of the point. Again, the bottom of the triangle extends only ¼" with the excess extending over the top of the point. DO NOT TRIM any excess fabric yet. Press seams away from point. Repeat 7 times.

3d Sew a point from step 2e sideways into the V completed in 3c. Pin at B then sew from A to B. Leaving needle in at B, lift presser foot, clip, then rotate. Continue sewing from B to C. Now trim excess triangle fabric. Press seams toward the V. Repeat 7 times.

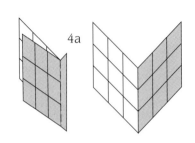

4a

4 Corner Point Construction

4a Pin two points from step 2e to each other at diamond intersections, then sew. Press. Repeat 3 times.

4b Pin a triangle from step 3a between the two points from 4a, then sew, with the triangle on top, from A to B. Leaving needle in at B, lift presser foot, clip, then rotate. Use seam ripper or tips of small scissors to help turn the fabric. Continue sewing from B to C. Triangle fabric will extend slightly beyond the point. Press. Repeat 3 times.

4c Pin a triangle to each outside edge of the piece completed in 4b, then sew. Press. Repeat 3 times.

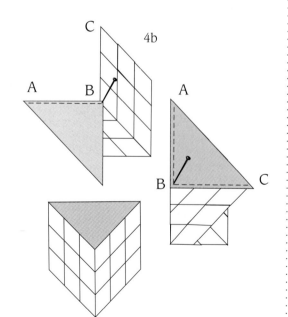

C
A B
4b
A
B C

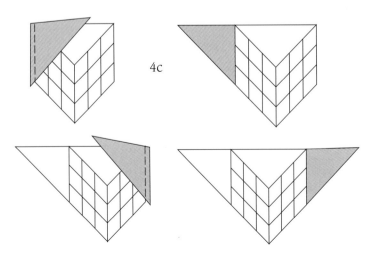

4c

5 Sewing Star Points

5a Pin two 3d points to each other, making sure that the horizontal points touch but do not overlap and the sides of the vertical points line up exactly, then sew. Press. Repeat 3 times.

5b Pin two pairs of points from 3d to each other, again making sure the horizontal points and the sides of the vertical points line up exactly, then sew. Press. Repeat.

5c Pin the two halves to each other, again making sure the horizontal and vertical points line up exactly.

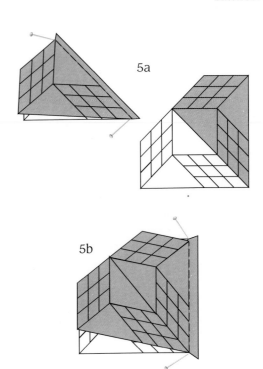

5a

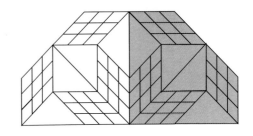

5b

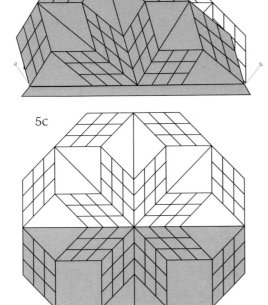

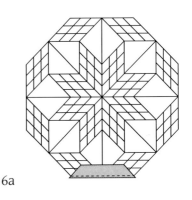

5c

6 Octagonal Border

Trim excess fabric evenly from each side. To ensure accuracy, measure each side as you go, add ½"; then cut a strip to the necessary length.

6a) Measure the first side. Add ½", then cut a 3½" strip of color C the necessary length. This first border strip will be the shortest of the eight. Pin, then sew. Press. (See insert A.)

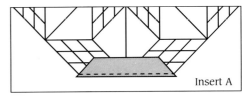

6a

Insert A

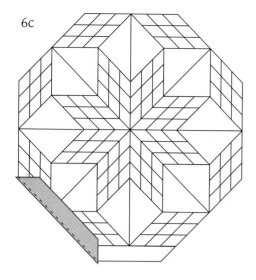

6c

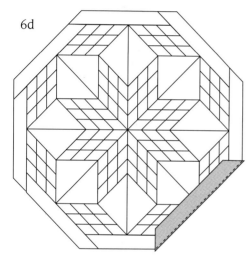

6d

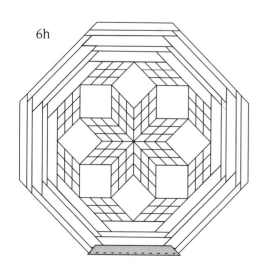

6h

6b With quilter's ruler, mark a 45° angle line across each end of this first strip (place the 45° angle line on the ruler parallel to the just-sewn seam; the cutting line is drawn along the side of ruler). Cut on the line.

6c Measure the next side; add ½". Cut a 3½" strip of color C the necessary length. Pin, then sew second border strip. Press. Mark a 45° angle line on each end of the just-sewn strip; cut. Working clockwise, repeat five times.

6d Measure the last side; add ½". Cut a 3½" strip of color C the necessary length. Pin, then sew. Press. Mark a 45° angle line on each end of the just-sewn strip; cut.

6e Starting in the same position as in 6a, measure the first side. Add ½", then cut a 2" strip of color B the necessary length. Pin, then sew. Press. For remaining strips repeat steps 6b through 6d, using color B and making each strip 2" wide.

6f Starting in the same position as in 6a, measure the first side. Add ½", then cut a 4" strip of color C the necessary length. Pin, then sew. Press. For remaining strips repeat steps 6b through 6d, using color C and making each strip 4" wide.

6g Starting in the same position as in 6a, measure the first side. Add ½", then cut a 2" strip of color B the necessary length. Pin, then sew. Press. For remaining strips repeat steps 6b through 6d, using color B and making each strip 2" wide.

6h Starting in the same position as in 6a, measure the first side. Add ½", then cut a 2½" strip of color C the necessary length. Pin, then sew. Press. The remaining strips of this series will be added to every other side, and each should be the same length. Cut, pin, then sew. Press.

7 Adding Corner Points

Pin a corner point from step 4c to a corner which does not have a 6h strip, then sew. Press. Repeat 3 times.

8) Border, quilting and binding directions are included in the basic instructions.

7

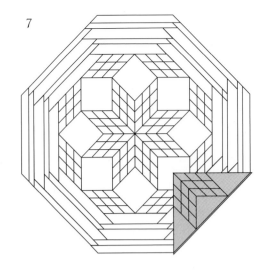

8

Linda Parker hand quilting. Beverly Magley, photo.

Original design made by Linda Parker for John Cartan and Betsy Brazy.

Variation of Bitterroot Star

Original design made by Linda Parker for Max's Testing. Marj Bourne photo

Bitterroot Star

Black Butterfly Star

Original design made by Linda Parker for Almira Jackson, named in honor of Jerry Belgarde.

Black Butterfly Star

✳

This quilt is named in honor of Jerry Belgarde. The design is simply a combination of Fast Star and Flying Swallow points. I first made a cream, rose and burgundy quilt of this design for Max Bourne. Later I made one in black, white, red and gray for Almira Jackson. The change in colors gave the appearance of an entirely different design.

Quilt size: 90"x 108"
Fabric:

A: Red: ½ yard
B: White print: ⅓ yard
C: Black: 3¾ yards
D: Dark gray: 4½ yards
E: Light gray: 3¼ yard
Quilt back: 6 yards color of choice
Binding: color C

1 Read through these directions before starting, then see basic instructions for cutting diamonds and squares. It is essential to cut the triangles 1½" larger than the point. When constructing the quilt top, pin/sew right sides together.

2 Small Point Construction

In this section two sets of small points will be made—AC and ABC.

2a Using diamond template size 2½"
Cut 112 diamonds Color A
Cut 64 diamonds Color B
Cut 112 diamonds Color C

2b Sew diamonds colors A & C together to make the first row of two diamonds. Repeat 79 times. Press half with seams toward color A and half with seams toward color C.

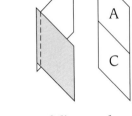

2c Sew two rows of diamonds together with color A at both points. Repeat 31 times. Press.

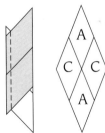

2d Sew two rows of diamonds together with color C at both points. Repeat 7 times. Press.

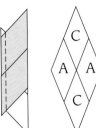

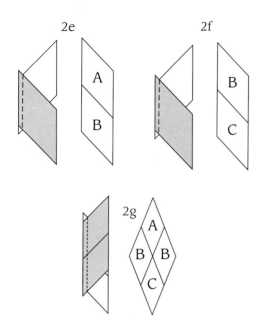

2e **Sew diamonds colors A & B together to make the first row of two diamonds. Repeat 31 times. Press seams toward color A.**

2f **Sew diamonds colors C & B together to make the second row. Repeat 31 times. Press seams toward color B.**

2g **Sew the two rows of diamonds together with color A at one point and color C at the other point. Press. Repeat 31 times.**

3 Small Fast Star Point Construction

Again, it is essential to always cut the triangles 1½" larger than the point. Even though they appear too large, this size is necessary for the horizontal point to fit. Also, measuring one side of a point, then adding 1½" always gives the accurate size of the square, which here should be 6".

3a **Cut 48, 6" squares of color D. Fold each square diagonally into two equal triangles. Press. Cut along the fold line.**

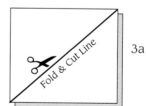

3b **Sew one short side of a triangle to the color C tip of a point from step 2g. Do not line up the edges evenly; rather, the triangle's bottom extends only ¼", with the excess extending over the top of the small point. DO NOT TRIM any excess fabric yet. Press seams away from point. Repeat 31 times.**

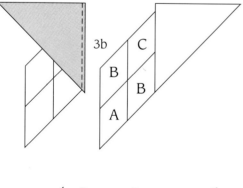

3c **Sew a second triangle to the opposite side of the color C tip of the point. Again, the bottom of the triangle only extends ¼" with the excess extending over the top of the small point. DO NOT TRIM any excess fabric yet. Press seams away from point. Repeat 31 times.**

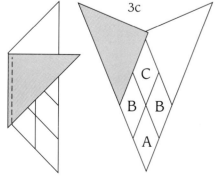

3d Sew a 2c point sideways into the V completed in 3c. Pin at B, then sew from A to B. Leaving needle in at B, lift presser foot, clip, then rotate. Continue sewing from B to C. Now trim excess triangle fabric. Press seams toward V. Repeat 7 times.

3e Sew another 3c piece to a completed 3d piece. Pin at B then sew from A to B. Leaving needle in at B, lift presser foot, clip, then rotate. Continue sewing from B to C. Now trim excess triangle fabric. Press seams toward V. Repeat 7 times. These are the eight outer fast star points.

3f Sew a point from 2d sideways into the V of a 3c piece as explained in 3d. Repeat 7 times.

3g Sew another 3c piece to a completed 3f piece, as explained in 3e. Repeat 7 times. These are the eight inner Fast Star points.

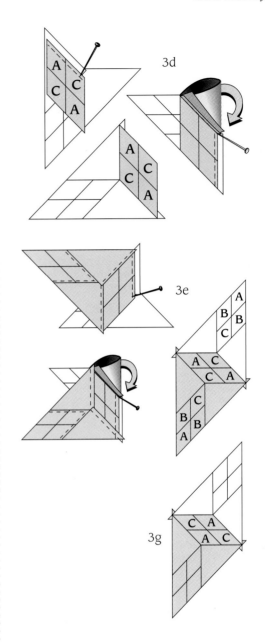

4 Flying Swallow Point Construction

4a Pin two points from step 2c to each other at diamond intersection, then sew. Press. Repeat 7 times.

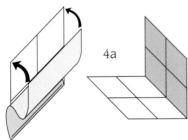

4b Pin another point from step 2c to the opposite side of a piece from 4a at diamond intersection; then sew. Press. Repeat 7 times.

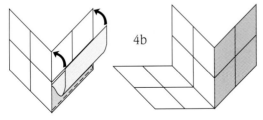

4c Pin triangle from 3b to a piece from 4b in between the points, then sew, with the triangle on top, from A to B. Leaving needle in at B, lift presser foot, clip, then rotate. Use seam ripper or tips of small scissors to help turn the fabric. Continue sewing from B to C. Triangle fabric will extend slightly beyond the point. Press. Repeat 7 times.

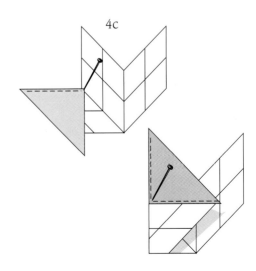

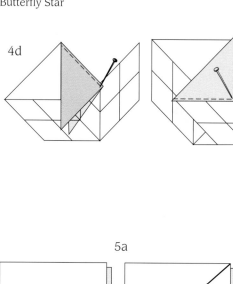

4d

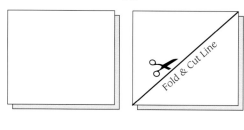

5a

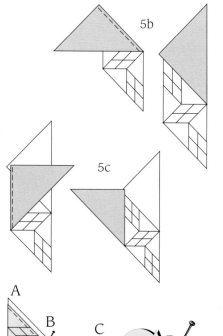

5b

5c

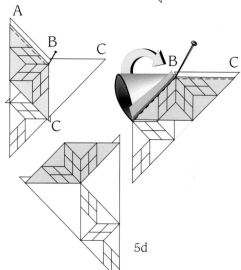

A

B C

C

C

5d

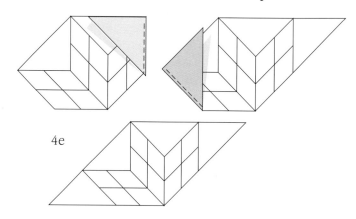

4d Repeat step 4c, placing triangle in between next two points.

4e Pin a triangle to each outside edge of the piece completed in 4d, then sew. Press. Repeat 7 times.

4e

5 Large Fast Star Point Construction

Again, it is essential to always cut the triangles 1½" larger than the point. Even though they appear too large, this size is necessary for the horizontal point to fit. Also, measuring one side of a point, then adding 1½" always gives the accurate size of the square, which here should be 12".

5a Cut 16, 13¼" squares of color E. Fold each square diagonally into two equal triangles. Press. Cut along the fold line.

5b Sew one short side of a triangle to a point from step 3e; similarly, sew another triangle to a point from step 3g. Do not line up the edges evenly; rather, the bottom of the triangle extends only ¼", with the excess extending over the top of the small point. **DO NOT TRIM** any excess fabric yet. Press seams away from point. Repeat 7 times for each type of point.

5c Sew a second triangle to the opposite side of each 5c point. Again, the bottom of the triangle extends only ¼" with the excess extending over the top of the point. **DO NOT TRIM** any excess fabric yet. Press seams away from point. Repeat 15 times.

5d Sew a 4e point sideways into the V completed in a 5d(3g) piece with the Flying Swallows diamond intersections toward the V. Pin at B then sew from A to B. Leaving needle in at B, lift presser foot, clip, then rotate. Continue sewing from B to C. Now trim excess triangle fabric. Press seams toward the V. Repeat 7 times.

5e Sew a 5d(3e) piece to a completed 5e piece with the center Flying Swallows point toward the V. Pin at B then sew from A to B. Leaving needle in B, lift presser foot, clip, then rotate. Continue sewing from B to C. Now trim excess triangle fabric. Press seams toward the V. Repeat 7 times.

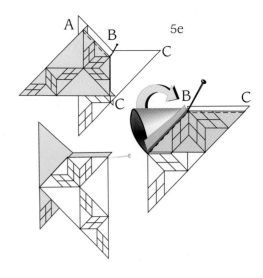

6   Sewing Star Points

The 5e(3g) points with the color C diamonds at the edges should be placed toward the center when sewing the points together. (For a different effect, the points can be all be reversed—the important thing is the 5e(3g) points must all be either toward the center or the outside.)

6a Pin two large points to each other, making sure the horizontal points touch but do not overlap and the sides of the vertical points line up exactly, then sew. Press. Repeat 3 times.

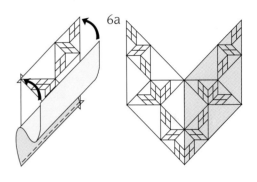

6b Pin two pairs of large points to each other, again making sure the horizontal points and the sides of the vertical points line up exactly, then sew. Press. Repeat.

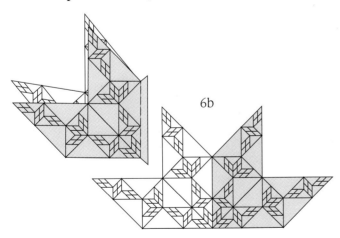

6c Pin the two halves to each other, again making sure the horizontal and vertical points line up exactly. Then sew the two halves. You may prefer to sew starting from the center, out. Press.

7c

7   Background Construction

7a Measure one side of a point, add 1". Cut two squares this size of color C and four of color D. Fold each square diagonally into two equal triangles. Press. Cut along the fold line.

7b Pin the color D triangle to the point, then sew, with the triangle on the top, from A to B. Leaving needle in at B, lift presser foot, clip, then rotate. Use seam ripper or tips of small scissors to help turn the fabric. Continue sewing from B to C. Triangle fabric will extend slightly beyond the point. Press. Repeat 7 times.

7c Sew long sides of color C triangles to the four corners. Press.

8   Border, quilting and binding directions are included in the basic instructions.

Variation of Black Butterfly Star quilt

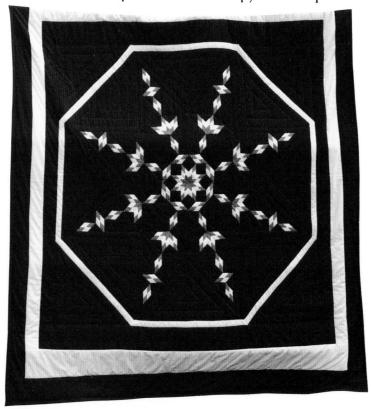

Original design made by Linda Parker for Max's Testing.
Black and White Photography, Billings, Mont., photo

Black Butterfly Star

Sweetgrass Star

Original design made by Linda Parker for Max's Testing. Marj Bourne photo

Sweetgrass Star

✳

Finished size: 89" X 106"
Fabric:
A: Burgundy print: 3 yards
B: Cream: 6 yards
C: Light Rose: ¾ yards
D: Burgundy: ¾ yards
Quilt back: 6 yards color of choice
Binding: color A or B

1   Read through these directions before starting, then see basic instructions for cutting diamonds and squares. It is essential to cut the triangles 1½" larger than the point. When constructing the quilt top, pin/sew right sides together.

2   Small Point Construction

2a Using diamond templates sizes 3½" and 8½"
Cut 80 diamonds Color A-3½"
Cut 16 diamonds Color D-8½"
Cut 80 diamonds Color C-3½"

2b Sew small diamonds color A & C together to make first row of two diamonds. Repeat 79 times. Press half with seams toward color A and half with seams toward color C.

2c Sew two rows of diamonds together with color A at both points. Repeat 39 times. Press.

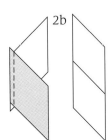
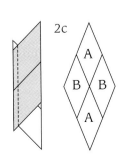

3   Half Point Construction

Again, it is essential to always cut the triangles 1½" larger than the point. Even though they appear too large, this size is necessary for the horizontal point to fit. Also, measuring one side of a point, then adding 1½" always gives the accurate size of the square, which here should be 8".

3a Cut 32, 8" squares of color B. Fold each square diagonally into two equal triangles. Press. Cut along the fold line.

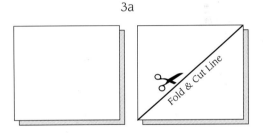

3b Sew one short side of a triangle to a point from step 2c. Do not line up the edges evenly; rather, the bottom of the triangle extends only ¼", with the excess extending over the top of the small point. **DO NOT TRIM** any excess fabric yet. Press seams away from point. Repeat 23 times.

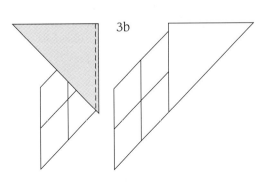

119

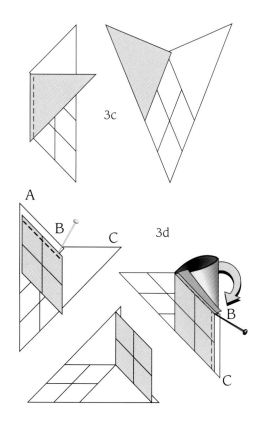

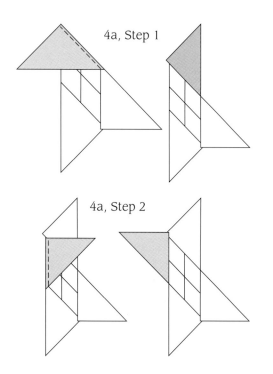

3c Sew a second triangle to the opposite side of the point. Again, the bottom of the triangle extends only ¼", with the excess extending over the top of the point. DO NOT TRIM any excess fabric yet. Press seams away from point. Repeat 23 times.

3d Sew another point from step 2c sideways into the V completed in 3c. Pin at B then sew from A to B. Leaving needle in at B, lift presser foot, clip, then rotate. Continue sewing from B to C. Now trim excess triangle fabric. Press seams toward the V. Repeat 15 times.

4 Large Point Construction

4a Sew short side of a triangle to each opposite side of a remaining 3c piece. Do not line up the edges evenly; rather, the bottom of the triangle extends only ¼", with the excess extending over the tip of the point. **DO NOT TRIM** any excess fabric yet. Press seams away from point. Repeat 7 times.

Original design made by Linda Parker for Max's Testing. Black and White Photography, Billings, Mont., photo

4b Sew a large color D diamond into the V in each side of a 4a piece. Pin at B then sew from A to B. Leaving needle in at B, lift presser foot, clip, then rotate. Continue sewing from B to C. Trim any excess fabric. Press. Repeat 7 times.

4b, Step 1

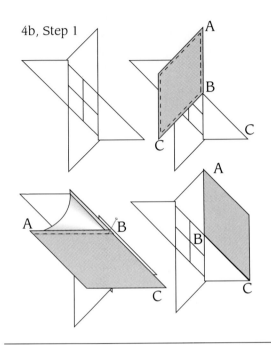

4c Sew a half Fast Star point from step 3d into the V on each end of a completed 4b piece. Pin at B then sew from A to B. Leaving needle in at B, lift presser foot, clip, then rotate. Continue sewing from B to C. Now trim excess triangle fabric. Press seams toward the V. Repeat 7 times.

4c, Step 1

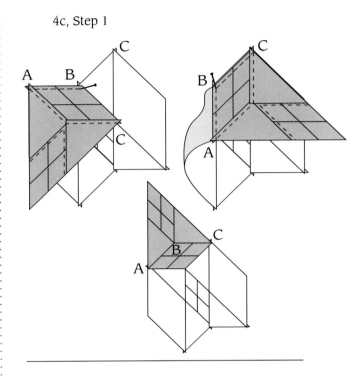

4b, Step 2

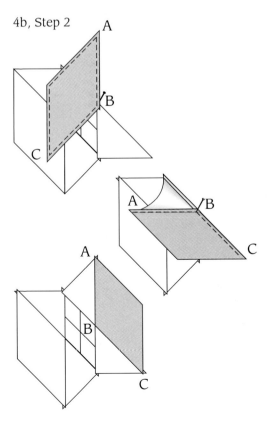

4c, Step 2

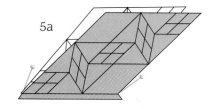

5a

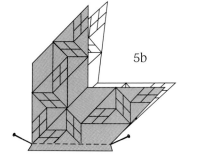

5b

5c

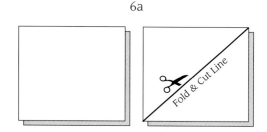

6a

5   Sewing Star Points

5a Pin two large points to each other, making sure the horizontal points touch but do not overlap and sides of the vertical points line up exactly, then sew. Press. Repeat 3 times.

5b Pin two pairs of large points to each other, again making sure the horizontal points and the sides of the vertical points line up exactly, then sew. Press. Repeat.

5c Pin the two halves to each other, again making sure the horizontal and vertical points line up exactly, then sew. You may prefer to sew starting from the center out. Press.

6   Background Construction

6a Measure one side of a point, add 1". Cut six squares this size of color B. Fold two squares diagonally into two equal triangles. Press. Cut

6b Pin a color B triangle to the point, then sew, with the triangle on the top, from A to B. Leaving needle in at B, lift presser foot, clip, then rotate. Continue sewing from B to C. Triangle fabric will extend slightly beyond the point. Press. Sew the remaining triangles, skipping every other space between points. Press.

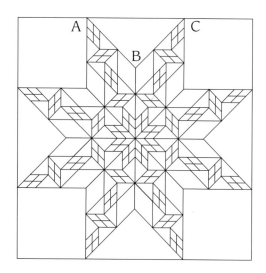

6c Sew the four background squares into the corners in the same manner.

7   Border, quilting and binding directions are included in the basic instructions.

Sweetgrass Star

Radiant Star

Original design made by Linda Parker.

Radiant Star

✳

The Radiant Star is a stunning display in nine shades of green.

Finished size: 90" X 108"

Fabric:

A: Darkest green: 4⅚ yards

B: Green: ⅙ yard

C: Green: ⅔ yards

D: Green: ¾ yards

E: Green: ½ yard

F: Green: ¼ yard

G: Green: ⅓ yard

H: Green: ⅔ yard

J: Lightest Green: ½ yard

Quilt back: 6 yards color of choice

Binding: color J.

1 **Read through these directions** before starting, then see basic instructions for cutting diamonds and squares. It is essential to cut the triangles 1½" larger than the point. When constructing the quilt top, pin/sew right sides together.

2 **Small Point Construction**

2a Using diamond template 3½"

Cut 8 diamonds A

Cut 16 diamonds B

Cut 8 diamonds C

Cut 24 diamonds D

Cut 48 diamonds E

Cut 24 diamonds F

Cut 40 diamonds G

Cut 80 diamonds H

Cut 40 diamonds J

3 **Small Point Construction**

The Radiant Star has three sets of points in varying shades of green. As a reference, each point is a three-shade combination, with the medium green on the sides, the lighter green at the top and the darker green at the bottom.

3a For the first set of small points: sew 2 diamonds, colors A & B together to make the first row of two diamonds. Press seams up. Repeat 7 times. Sew diamonds, colors B & C together to make the second row. Press seams up. Repeat 7 times. Pin at diamond intersection with color C at the top and color A at the bottom, then sew. Press. Repeat 7 times.

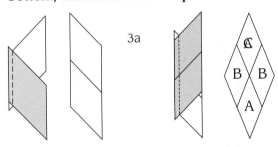

3a

3b For the second set of small points: sew 2 diamonds, colors D & E together to make the first row. Press seams up. Repeat 23 times. Sew diamonds, colors E & F together to make the second row. Press seams up. Repeat 23 times. Pin at diamond intersections with color F at the top and color D at the bottom, then sew. Press. Repeat 23 times.

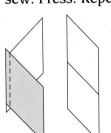 3b

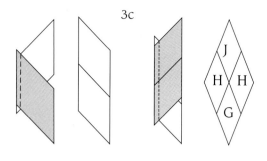

3c

3c For the third set of points: sew 2 diamonds, colors G & H together to make the first row. Press seams up. Repeat 39 times. Sew diamonds, colors H & J together to make the second row. Press seams up. Repeat 39 times. Pin at diamond intersections with color J at the top and color G at the bottom, then sew. Press. Repeat 39 times.

4 Point Construction

The Radiant Star is sewn together in 8 identical sections. There are two sizes of triangles, the larger triangles on the first and second sets of points, and the smaller triangles on the outer set of points.

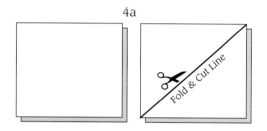

4a

4a Cut 24, 7" squares of color A. Fold each square diagonally into two equal triangles. Press. Cut along the fold line. These are the triangles for the inner sets of points.

4b Cut 12, 7½" squares of color A. Fold each square diagonally into two equal triangles. Press. Cut along fold line. Fold each triangle in half. Press and cut along fold line. These are the triangles for the outer set of points.

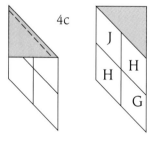

4c

4c Sew long side of a triangle from 4b to the top right side of a point from 3c (GHHJ). Do not line up the edges evenly; rather, the bottom of the triangle extends only ¼", with the excess extending over the top of the small point. **DO NOT TRIM** any excess fabric yet. Press seams away from point. Repeat 23 times.

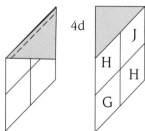

4d

4d Sew long side of a triangle from 4b to the top left side of another point from 3c (GHHJ). Do not line up the edges evenly; rather, the bottom of the triangle extends only ½", with the excess extending over the top of the small point. DO NOT TRIM any excess fabric yet. Press seams away from point. Repeat 15 times.

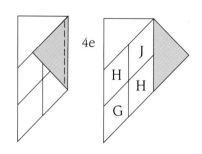

4e

4e Sew long side of a triangle from 4b to the opposite top side of a point from 4d. Do not line up the edges evenly; rather, the bottom of the triangle extends only ¼", with the excess extending over the top of the small point. **DO NOT TRIM** any excess fabric yet. Press seam up. Repeat 7 times.

4f Sew one short side of a triangle from 4a to the opposite bottom side of a remaining 4d piece. Do not line up the edges evenly; rather, the top of the triangle extends only ½", with the excess extending over the bottom of the small point. **DO NOT TRIM** any excess fabric yet. Press. Repeat 15 times.

4g Sew one short side of a triangle from 4a to the opposite bottom side of a 4c piece. Do not line up the edges evenly; rather, the top of the triangle extends only ½", with the excess extending over the bottom of the small point. **DO NOT TRIM** any excess fabric yet. Press. Repeat 15 times.

4h Sew a point from 3b to the short side of the bottom triangle on a 4f piece, with color F at the top. Press. Repeat 15 times.

4i Sew a point from 3b to the short side of the bottom triangle on a 4g piece, with color F at the top. Press. Repeat 7 times.

4j Sew one short side of a triangle from 4a to the opposite bottom side of a 4h piece. Do not line up the edges evenly; rather, the top of the triangle extends only ½", with the excess extending over the bottom of the small point. **DO NOT TRIM** any excess fabric yet. Press. Repeat 7 times.

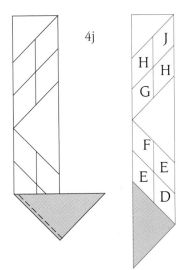

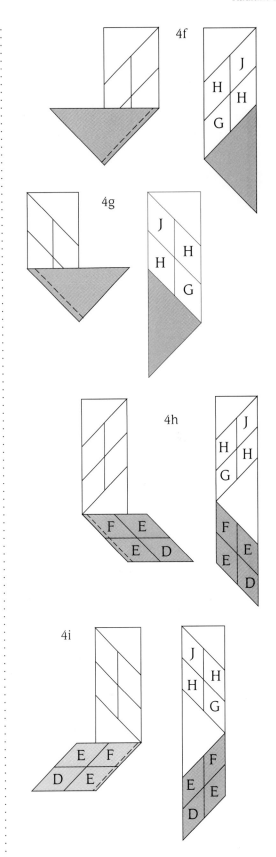

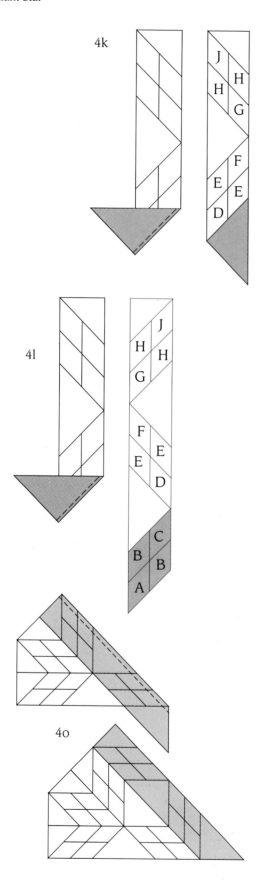

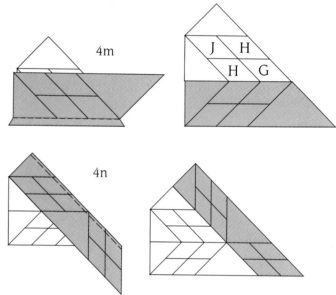

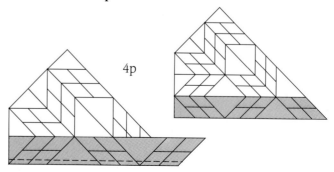

4k Sew one short side of a triangle from 4a to the opposite bottom side of a 4i piece. Do not line up the edges evenly; rather, the top of the triangle extends only ½", with the excess extending over the bottom of the small point. **DO NOT TRIM** any excess fabric yet. Press. Repeat 7 times.

4l Sew a point from 3a to the short side of the bottom triangle on a 4j piece, with color C at the top. Press. Repeat 7 times.

4m Pin a 4g piece to a 4e piece at diamond intersections, then sew. Press. Repeat 7 times.

4n Pin a 4h piece to the 4e side of a 4m piece at diamond intersections, then sew. Press. Repeat 7 times.

4o Pin a 4j piece to the right side of a 4n piece at diamond intersections, then sew. Press. Repeat 7 times.

4p Pin a 4l piece to the opposite side of a 4o piece at 3c and 3b point diamond intersections, then sew. Press. Repeat 7 times.

5 Sewing Star Points

5a Pin two large points (from 4p) to each other at diamond intersections, then sew. Press. Repeat 3 times.

5b Pin two pairs of points to each other at diamond intersections, then sew. Press. Repeat.

5c Pin the two halves to each other at diamond intersections, then sew. You may prefer to sew starting from the center, out. Press.

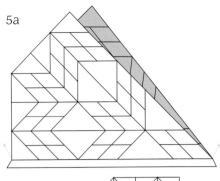

5a

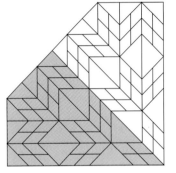

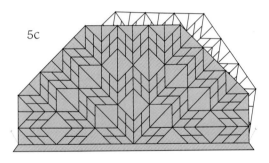

5c

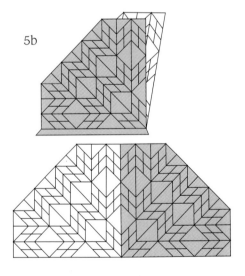

5b

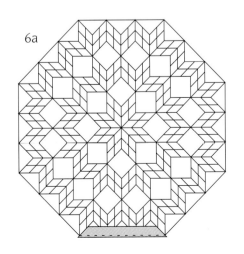

6a

6 Octagonal Border

Trim excess fabric evenly from each side. To ensure accuracy, measure each side as you go; add ½" for seam allowance, then cut a strip the necessary length.

6a Measure the first side. Add ½", then cut a 3" strip of color A the necessary length. This first border strip will be the shortest of the eight. Pin, then sew. Press.

6c

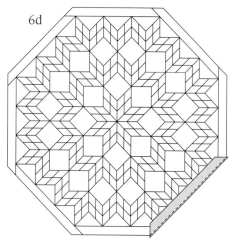

6d

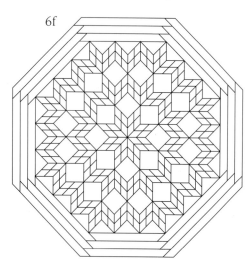

6f

6b With quilter's ruler, mark a 45° angle line across each end of this first strip (place the 45° angle line on the ruler parallel to the just-sewn seam; the cutting line is drawn along the side of ruler). Cut on the line.

6c Measure the next side; add ½". Cut a 3" strip of color A the necessary length. Pin, then sew second border strip. Press. Mark a 45° angle line on each end of the just-sewn strip; cut. Working clockwise, repeat five times.

6d Measure the last side; add ½". Cut a 3" strip of color A the necessary length. Pin, then sew. Press. Mark a 45° angle line on each end of the just-sewn strip; cut.

6e Starting in the same position as in 6a, measure the first side. Add ½", then cut a 3" strip of color J the necessary length. Pin, then sew. Press. For remaining strips repeat steps 6b through 6d, using color J and making each strip 3" wide.

6f Starting in the same position as in 6a, measure the first side. Add ½", then cut a 3" strip of color A the necessary length. Pin, then sew. Press. For remaining strips repeat steps 6b through 6d, using color A and making each strip 3" wide.

7 Adding Corner Triangles

7a Lay quilt top on the floor. Using two yardsticks, square off a corner. Measure from A to B, then add ½" for seam allowance. Cut two squares this size of color A. Fold each square diagonally into two equal triangles. Press. Cut along the fold line.

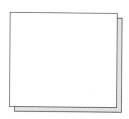 

Fold & Cut Line

7b Sew long sides of color A triangles to the four corners. Press.

7c For those of you who are mathematically inclined, the formula for this square (without the ½" seam allowance) is one you learned in high school: "the square of the hypotenuse of a right triangle (c^2) is equal to the sum of the squares of the other two sides (a^2+b^2)." In other words, you could measure one octagonal side, square that, divide that number in half (because this is a square, each other side of the right triangle is the same length), and then take the square root of that number. I find it much easier to use the yardstick method!

8 Border, quilting and binding directions are included in the basic instructions.

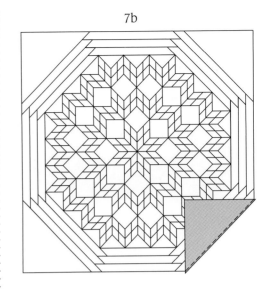

7b

Original design made by Linda Parker for Max's Testing. Black and White Photography, Billings, Mont., photo

Radiant Star Variation

Original design made by Linda Parker.

Radiant Star

Kaleidoscope

Original design made by Linda Parker

Kaleidoscope Star

✳

This design is simply a combination of the Fast Star and the Lone Star. Although piecing the top takes about 40 hours—it is much easier than it looks.

Finished size 90" x102"
Fabric:
A: Red: 2⅓ yards
B: Turquoise: 1⅚ yards
C: Purple: 2⅔ yards
D: Yellow: 3⅙ yards
E: Teal: 1⅓ yards
Quilt back: 6 yards color of choice
Binding: excess of color A, B, C or D

1 **Read through these directions** before starting, then see basic instructions for cutting diamonds and squares. It is essential to cut the triangles 1½" larger than the point. When constructing the quilt top, pin/sew right sides together.

2 **Small Point Construction**

2a Using diamond template size 3½"
    Cut 144 diamonds Color A
    Cut 72 diamonds Color B

2b Square size 5"
    Cut 72 squares Color C
    Cut 72 squares Color D

2c Fold each square diagonally into two equal triangles. Press. Cut along fold line.

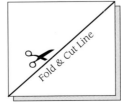

2d Sew one short side of a triangle color D to a color A diamond. Do not line up the edges evenly; rather, the bottom of the triangle extends only ¼", with the excess extending over the top of the diamond. **DO NOT TRIM** any excess fabric yet. Press seam away from diamond. Repeat 71 times.

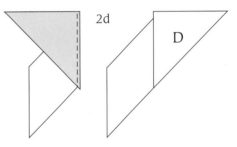

2e Sew a second color D triangle to the opposite side of the diamond. Again, the bottom of the triangle extends only ¼" with the excess extending over the top of the diamond. **DO NOT TRIM** any excess fabric yet. Press seam away from diamond. Repeat 71 times.

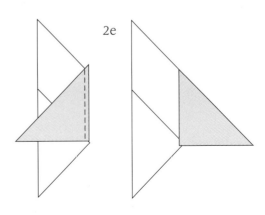

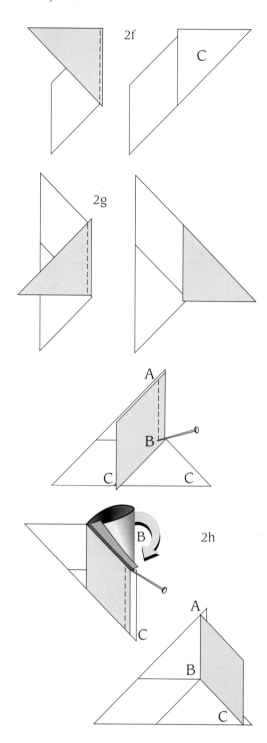

2f

C

2g

A

B

C   C

B

2h

A

B

C

2i/completed point

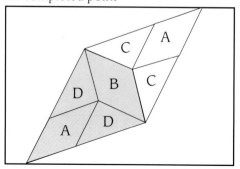

C   A

C

D   B   C

A   D

2f Sew one short side of a triangle color C to a color A diamond. Do not line up the edges evenly; rather, the bottom of the triangle extends only ¼", with the excess extending over the top of the diamond. **DO NOT TRIM** any excess fabric yet. Press seam away from diamond. Repeat 71 times.

2g Sew a second color C triangle to the opposite side of the diamond. Again, the bottom of the triangle extends only ¼" with the excess extending over the top of the diamond. **DO NOT TRIM** any excess fabric yet. Press seams away from the diamond. Repeat 71 times.

Keep the 2e and 2g pieces in separate piles to ensure they are not inadvertently used in the wrong order.

2h Sew a color B diamond sideways into the V completed in 2e. Pin at B then sew from A to B. Leaving needle in at B, lift presser foot, clip, then rotate. Continue sewing from B to C. Now trim excess triangle fabric. Press seams toward the V. Repeat 71 times.

2i) Sew a 2g piece to a completed 2h piece. Pin at B then sew from A to B. Leaving needle in at B, lift presser foot, clip, then rotate. Continue sewing from B to C. Now trim excess triangle fabric. Press seams toward the V. Repeat 71 times.

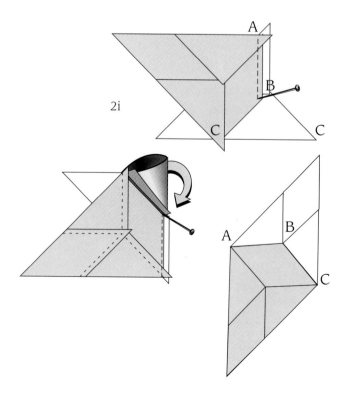

A

B

C   C

2i

A   B

A

C

3   Large Point Construction

When sewing the small points into rows, and the rows to each other, the 2e tips should be pointing in the same direction. When sewing the small points into rows, treat each small point as if it were a diamond, and note that there are no diamond intersections to line up.

3a Sew the first row of small points from the top to the bottom. Press.

3b Sew the second row of small points from the top to the bottom. Press. Pin second row to first row, making sure the horizontal diamonds within the small points touch but do not overlap, then sew. Press.

3c Sew the third row of small points from the top to the bottom. Press. Pin third row to second row, making sure the horizontal diamonds within the small points touch but do not overlap, then sew. Press.

3d Repeat 3a through 3c 7 times.

4   Sewing Star Points

4a Pin two large points to each other, making sure the tips of the horizontal diamonds touch but **do not** overlap, then sew. Press. Repeat 3 times.

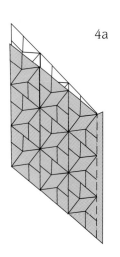

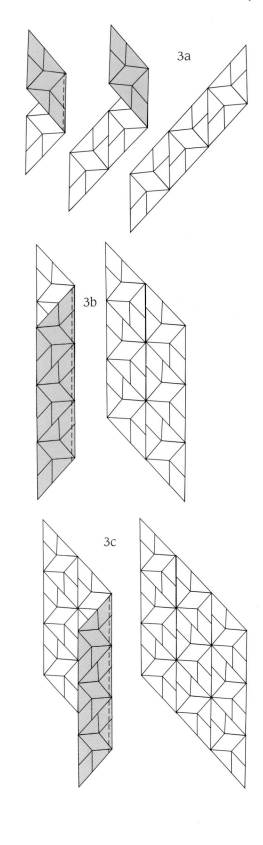

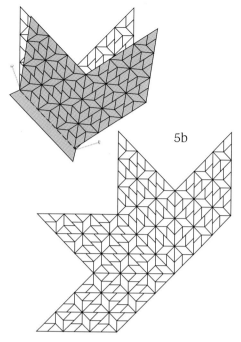

5b

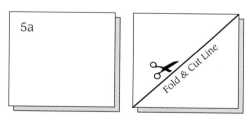

Original design made by Linda Parker for Max's testing. Marj Bourne photo

5a

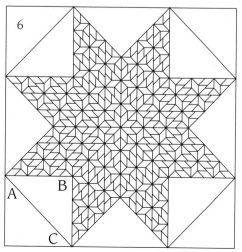

Fold & Cut Line

6

A B

C

4b Pin two pairs of large points to each other, again making sure the tips of the horizontal diamonds touch but do not overlap; then sew. Press. Repeat.

4c Pin the two halves to each other, again making sure the tips of the horizontal diamonds touch but do not overlap. Then sew the two halves. You may prefer to sew starting from the center out. Press.

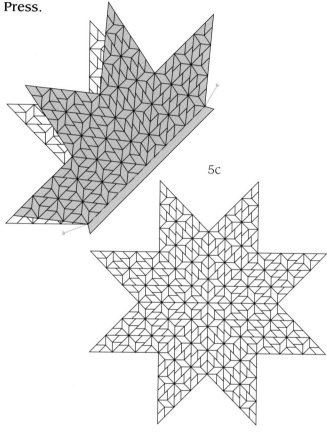

5c

5 Background Construction

5a Measure one side of a point, add 1 inch. Cut two squares this size of color D and four of color E. Fold each square diagonally into two equal triangles. Press. Cut along the fold line.

5b Pin a color E triangle to the point, then sew, with the triangle on the top, from A to B. Leaving needle in at B, lift presser foot, clip, then rotate. Continue sewing from B to C. Triangle fabric will extend slightly beyond the point. Press. Repeat 7 times.

5c Sew long sides of color D triangles to the four corners. Press.

6 Border, quilting and binding directions are included in the basic instructions.

Kaleidoscope Star

Original design made by Linda Parker

Original design made by Linda Parker for Max's testing. Marj Bourne photo

Josh's Star

Original design made by Linda Parker

Josh's Star

✳

This makes a great wall hanging or pillow top . . . and it can be finished in an afternoon, or in an evening.

Finished size: 25" x 25½"
Fabric:
A: Burgundy print: 16"
B: Blue: 8½"
C: Cream: 3½"
D: Dusty Rose: 10½"
 Quilt back: 27" square color of choice
Binding: 12" color of choice

1 **Read through these directions** before starting, then see basic instructions for cutting diamonds and squares. It is essential to cut the triangles 1½" larger then the point. When constructing the quilt top, pin/sew right sides together.

2 **Point Construction**

2a Using diamond template sizes 2" and 3½"

   Cut 32 diamonds color C-2"
   Cut 16 diamonds color B-2"
   Cut 16 diamonds color D-2"
   Cut 16 diamonds color A-3½"

2b Sew diamonds, colors B & C, together to make the first row of two diamonds. Repeat 15 times. Press seams toward color B.

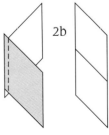

2c Sew diamonds, colors D & C, together to make the second row of two diamonds. Repeat 15 times. Press seams toward color D.

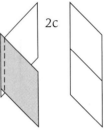

2d Sew two rows of diamonds together with color B at one point and color D at the other point. Repeat 15 times. Press.

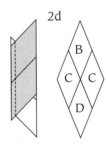

2e Sew a large color A diamond to a point from 2d. Repeat 15 times. Press half with seams toward color A and half with seams in the opposite direction.

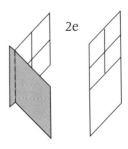

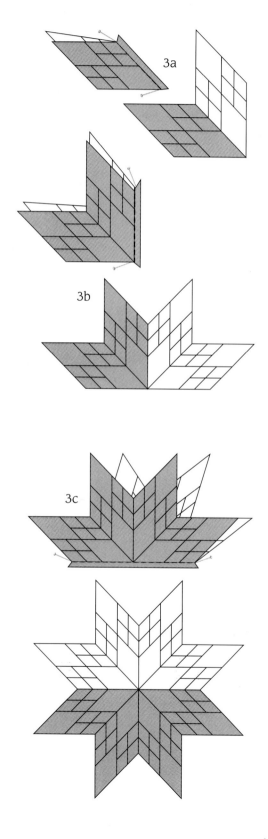

2f Sew two rows of diamonds from step 2e together with color A at both points. Repeat 7 times. Press.

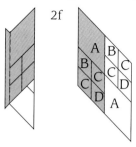

3 Sewing Star Points

3a Pin two points to each other at diamond intersections, then sew. Press. Repeat 3 times.

3b Pin two pairs of points to each other at diamond intersections, then sew. Press. Repeat.

3c Pin the two halves to each other at diamond intersections, then sew. You may prefer to sew starting from the center, out. Press.

Original design variation made by Linda Parker

4 Background Construction

4a Measure one side of a point, then add 1". Cut 6 squares this size of color D. Fold two squares diagonally into two equal triangles. Press. Cut along the fold line.

4b Pin a color D triangle to the point, then sew, with the triangle on the top, from A to B. Leaving needle in at B, lift presser foot, clip, then rotate. Continue sewing from B to C. Triangle fabric will extend slightly beyond the point. Press. Sew the remaining triangles, skipping every other space between points. Press.

4c Sew the four background squares into the corners in the same manner. Press.

4c

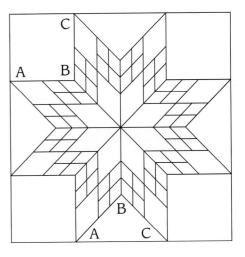

5 Border Construction

Always measure each side as you go, eliminating any potential error in the lengths of the strips. Add ½" to these measurements. Excess fabric can always be trimmed; not enough requires more measuring and piecing.

5a Measure one side of the finished top. Cut two strips of color B 2½" x 19½"; cut two more strips, 2½" x 24½" (24½" equals 19½" plus 5" which is the width of the previous two strips). Sew the two 19½" strips to the sides. Press. Then sew the 24½" strips to the top and bottom. Press.

5b For the second border strip, color A: cut two strips 2½" x 24½", and two strips 2½" x 29½". Sew the two 24½" strips to the sides. Press. Then sew the 29½" strips to the top and bottom. Press.

6 Quilting and binding directions are included in the basic instructions.

Variation of Josh's Star

Original design variation made by Linda Parker

Variation of Josh's Star

✳

The quilts pictured have the same number of diamonds; the small and large diamonds are simply reversed. This is a good example of the ease with which you can create different effects through rearranging diamonds.

Finished size: 23" X 23"

Fabric:

A: Dark blue: 6"

B: Tan: 3½"

C: Brown/blue/tan print: 8½"

D: Light blue: 7"

Quilt back: 26" square color of choice

Binding: 12" color of choice

Follow the directions for Josh's Star quilt in the previous chapter exactly except for 2a-2f, which are repeated below with the necessary changes.

2a Using diamond template size 2" and 3½"

   Cut 32 diamonds color C-2"

   Cut 32 diamonds color B-2"

   Cut 16 diamonds color A-3½"

2b Sew diamonds, colors B & C, together to make the first row of two diamonds. Repeat 31 times. Press seams toward color B.

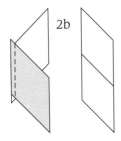

2c Sew two rows of diamonds together with color C at both points. Repeat 15 times. Press.

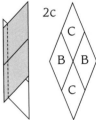

2d Sew a large color A diamond to a point from 2c. Repeat 15 times. Press half with seams toward color A and half with seams in the opposite direction.

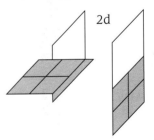

2e Sew two rows of diamonds from step 2d together with small point from step 2b at both points. Repeat 7 times. Press.

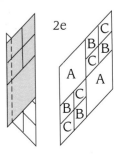

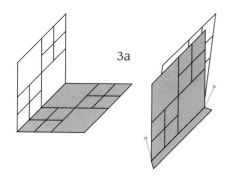

3a

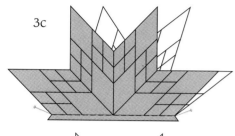

3c

4c

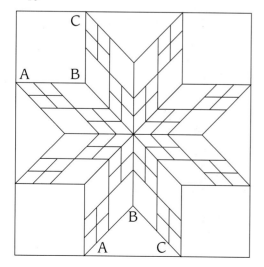

3 Sewing Star Points

3a Pin two points to each other at diamond intersections, then sew. Press. Repeat 3 times.

3b Pin two pairs of points to each other at diamond intersections, then sew. Press. Repeat.

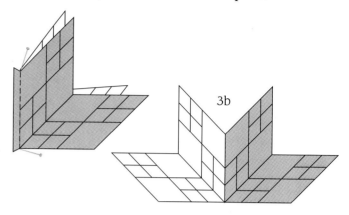

3b

3c Pin the two halves to each other at diamond intersections, then sew. You may prefer to sew starting from the center, out. Press.

4 Background Construction

4a Measure one side of a point, then add 1". Cut 6 squares this size of color D. Fold two squares diagonally into two equal triangles. Press. Cut along the fold line.

4b Pin a color D triangle to the point, then sew, with the triangle on the top, from A to B. Leaving needle in at B, lift presser foot, clip, then rotate. Continue sewing from B to C. Triangle fabric will extend slightly beyond the point. Press. Sew the remaining triangles, skipping every other space between points. Press.

4c Sew the four background squares into the corners in the same manner. Press.

5 Border Construction

Always measure each side as you go, eliminating any potential error in the lengths of the strips. Add ½" to these measurements. Excess fabric can always be trimmed; not enough requires more measuring and piecing.

5a Measure one side of the finished top. Cut two strips of color B 2½" x 19½"; cut two more strips, 2½" x 24½" (24½" equals 19½" plus 5" which is the width of the previous two strips). Sew the two 19½" strips to the sides. Press. Then sew the 24½" strips to the top and bottom. Press.

5b For the second border strip, color A, cut two strips 2½" x 24½", and two strips 2½" x 29½". Sew the two 24½" strips to the sides. Press. Then sew the 29½" strips to the top and bottom. Press.

6 Quilting and binding directions are included in the basic instructions.

Original design variation made by Linda Parker

Josh's Star

Josh's Variation

＊

Beams of light radiate

In the late afternoon.

I watch her hands

And needle flashing

weaving in and out.

For eighteen years

Her fingers have done this,

In and out, pieced...and bled.

Sioux and Assiniboine have done this

for generations before on buffalo robes.

For give-aways and celebrations

Most honorable item

Given or received.

Warriors returning from battle,

Maidens getting married.

Even when she has gone, I'll always remember,

My mother and her wonderful Star Quilts.

by Jennifer Hedges

"Grandma's Legacy" by Winnie Ore, watercolor

Biography

✳

Almira Jackson, a nationally known and highly respected star quilter, lives on the Fort Peck Reservation in Montana. An Assiniboine, she was born March 8, 1917 south of the Frazer school in a log house. Almira has been making quilts most of her life, and says she has made thousands of quilts. Almira (Grandma Snail) loves to exaggerate. In reality, if she has made an average of one a week for 50 years, she has made at least 2,600 quilts, perhaps more.

Jeanne Oyawin Eder, an enrolled member of the Santee Sioux tribe, has been a professor of Native American Studies at Eastern Montana College in Billings, Montana, and is presently the Multi-cultural Coordinator at Western Montana College of the University of Montana, Dillon, Montana.

Jerry Belgard, a Chippewa, was adopted into the Red Bottom Clan of the Assiniboine Sioux. She is the Director of Title V/Indian Education for the Billings, Montana Public Schools.

Florence Vande Sandt, born in North Dakota and raised in a German farming community north of Gildford, Montana, now resides in Havre, Montana. She is Linda Parker's maternal grandmother. She has made many quilts during her full and lengthy life.

Brigit A. Fast Horse, a Sioux, passed away June 14, 1996 in Wolf Point after a long battle with cancer. She was one of the best Star Quilters on the Fort Peck Reservation.

Eddie Barbeau, an Ojibway, was born on the Fort Berthold Reservation in North Dakota, and grew up with his grandparents on the White Earth Reservation in Minnesota. For decades he was the ceremonial leader for all Helena Indians. A hero of World War II, he was also an elder, pipe holder and shield keeper. He died in 1994 in Helena, Montana.

Bibliography

✳

The Sacred Pipe, Black Elk's Account of the Seven Rites of the Oglala Sioux, Recorded and Edited by Joseph Epes Brown, First published as Volume 36 in The Civilization of the American Indian Series by the University of Oklahoma Press in 1953, Penguin Books, Inc. 1971.

Lame Deer Seeker of Visions, John (Fire) Lame Deer and Richard Erdoes, Washington Square Press, Simon & Schuster, 1972.

The Hidden Half: Studies of Plains Indian Women, Patricia Albers and Beatrice Medicine, University Press of America, 1983.

Black Elk Speaks: Being the Life Story of a Holy Man of the Oglala Sioux, as told through John G. Neihardt (Flaming Rainbow), original copyright 1932 by John G. Neihardt, University of Nebraska Press, Lincoln and London, 1989.

Crying for a Dream: The World Through Native American Eyes, Richard Erdoes, Bear & Company, Santa Fe, New Mexico, 1990.

"My Grandmother's Star Quilt Honors Me," Jeanne Oyawin Eder, Nancy Tucker, Montana Committee for the Humanities, Box 8036 Hellgate Station, Missoula, Montana, 1980.

Teaching from the American Earth, Indian Religion and Philosophy. Dennis Tedlock and Barbara Tedlock. New York: Liveright Publishing Corp.,1975. p. 216.

Flynn Quilt Frame Company, 1000 Shiloh Overpass Road, Billings, Montana 59106 (406) 656-8986.